ZIMBABWE
A Break with the Past?
Human Rights and Political Unity

AN AFRICA WATCH REPORT

October 1989

485 Fifth Avenue
New York, NY 10017
(212) 972-8400

1522 K Street, N.W.
Washington, DC 20005
(202) 371-6592

90 Borough High Street
London SE1 1LL
England
378-8008

This report was written by Richard Carver, Research Director of Africa Watch. It is based on research carried out between April and September 1989, including a visit to Zimbabwe in April.

THE AFRICA WATCH COMMITTEE

The Africa Watch Committee was established in May 1988 to monitor and promote observance of internationally recognized human rights in Africa. The Executive Director is Rakiya Omaar, the Research Director is Richard Carver and Joyce Mends-Cole is the Washington Representative.

HUMAN RIGHTS WATCH

Human Rights Watch comprises Africa Watch, Americas Watch, Asia Watch, Helsinki Watch and Middle East Watch. The Chairman is Robert L. Bernstein, the Vice Chairman is Adrian W. DeWind. The Executive Director is Aryeh Neier and Kenneth Roth is Deputy Director. For further information, including a full publications list with subscription forms or an annual report, please write to:

Human Rights Watch	Human Rights Watch
485 Fifth Avenue	1522 K Street, N.W.
New York, NY 10017	Washington, DC 20005
FAX (212) 972-0905	FAX (202) 371-0124
Attn: Publications Coordinator	Attn: Publications Coordinator

Table of Contents

1. INTRODUCTION

Zimbabwe became independent nearly a decade ago in the least favorable of circumstances. For 90 years of colonial rule, a white settler government had strictly enforced a system of rigid racial discrimination and political disenfranchisement of the majority black population. For the last eight years or so of colonial rule the country was torn by a war of independence. Hundreds of black nationalists were detained from the early 1960s and the Rhodesian army brutally repressed the rural population.

This appalling legacy should not be forgotten in any discussion of Zimbabwe's human rights record since independence — nor should the grave security threats the country has suffered. South Africa has launched overt military raids and covert sabotage operations against Zimbabwe, at the same time as supplying arms to surrogate organizations fighting the government. It has not been the easiest of situations in which to cultivate respect for human rights.

However, it is not by the poor standards of the pre-independence regimes that Zimbabwe's human rights record should be judged — nor would the government wish it to be. Since independence Zimbabwe has become party to international human rights treaties, notably the African Charter on Human and Peoples' Rights. This is an indication of the standards to which the Zimbabwean Government aspires and it is by such internationally accepted norms that this report reviews its record.

This report is published at the present time not because Zimbabwe's recent observance of human rights has been especially poor — indeed the government has made significant improvements in recent years in response to local and international criticism. However, with the stated desire to move towards a one-party political system and a new mood of unity at the national level, this is a suitable moment to review the lessons of Zimbabwe's troubled recent history and to suggest ways in which safeguards against abuse can be built

1

into the political and constitutional system. More particularly Zimbabwe faces a serious security threat along its eastern border with Mozambique. Guerrillas of the Resistencia Nacional Mocambicana (Mozambique National Resistance — RENAMO or MNR) have been responsible for many brutal attacks, ostensibly in reaction to the deployment of the Zimbabwean army in support of the Government of Mozambique. Also in the eastern part of the country there have been bitter peasant struggles over land and, in recent months, the emergence of a new political party committed to military withdrawal from Mozambique and a solution to the land question. Confronted with a similar situation in Matabeleland in the early 1980s — South African-backed insurgency, economic grievances and political opposition — the security forces responded by perpetrating gross human rights abuses. The Matabeleland crisis is over. The government has put an end to serious abuses and reached a political solution to the conflict. However, the crucial question is whether the lessons of Matabeleland have been learned — or whether that human rights emergency is destined to be repeated in eastern Zimbabwe.

This report briefly reviews the history of human rights abuses before independence and in the early 1980s. However, its principal focus is on the period since December 1987, when the two main political parties, the Zimbabwe African National Union-Patriotic Front (ZANU-PF) and the Zimbabwe African People's Union (ZAPU) — concluded a unity agreement which prepared the way for an end to the Matabeleland conflict. The report reviews the application of an amnesty in 1988 for armed opponents of the government, as well as members of the security forces imprisoned for human rights abuses. It considers the government's response to international reports of torture by Zimbabwean police and intelligence — documenting the general improvement in treatment of prisoners, but also presenting new evidence of continuing torture by the Central Intelligence Organization (CIO).

This report also examines the legal background to human rights abuses in Zimbabwe, principally the continuing State of Emergency which empowers the government to detain without trial. We document current cases of detention without trial, as well as some instances of police interference in the administration of justice.

2

In recent months there has been a mushrooming of public criticism of the government — through press reporting of corruption, student demonstrations and the formation of a new political party. The report reviews the government's somewhat uneven response to popular opposition.

The report documents the gross abuses committed by RENAMO in eastern Zimbabwe, but also criticizes the counterinsurgency tactics of the Zimbabwean army on both sides of the border. In particular we document serious violations of international law in the forced removal of Mozambicans from their country and the forcible return of refugees across the Mozambique border.

The report concludes with Africa Watch's recommendations to the government for reforms to safeguard human rights in the future, as well as a review of United States policy towards Zimbabwe.

2. THE LEGACY — INDEPENDENCE AND THE MATABELELAND CRISIS

Rhodesia (more properly the British colony of Southern Rhodesia) was founded upon an institutionalized form of racial discrimination not unlike the apartheid system in neighboring South Africa. Blacks, who made up the overwhelming majority of the population, were excluded from political power and were only allowed to farm land in designated areas. At independence the rural areas were divided almost equally between European and African land — 18 million hectares apiece. Yet there were roughly one hundred times as many African farmers as whites and African-designated land was almost exclusively in the regions with poorer soil and rainfall.

Any attempt to challenge the status quo by non-violent political methods was met with repression. In the early 1960s ZAPU and ZANU were banned and their leaders, including Robert Mugabe and Joshua Nkomo, detained without trial. In November 1965 the government declared a State of Emergency, which gave it powers to detain opponents without trial. Hundreds of Zimbabwean nationalists were imprisoned under emergency powers, many for years at a time. On November 11, 1965, a few days after introducing the state of emergency, the Rhodesian Front government led by Ian Smith made a Unilateral Declaration of Independence (UDI) from Britain, which signalled an increase in the repression of black nationalism and an end to any hope of peaceful constitutional reform. In the late 1960s the nationalist parties launched an armed struggle against the (technically illegal) Rhodesian regime, which from 1972 onwards developed into a major bush war.

The regime used increasingly brutal methods to suppress nationalist agitation. The scope of the death penalty was dramatically extended and there were dozens of secret executions of opponents. Torture was systematic and widespread, and included beatings, electric shocks and immersion in water until the victim lost consciousness.

5

The security forces responded to the bush war by indiscriminate measures against the rural population. Three-quarters of a million rural Zimbabweans were moved into 220 protected villages (PVs). The idea, which originated with the British in Malaya, practiced by the United States in Vietnam, and has also been followed by several other governments in devising counter-insurgent strategies, was to isolate the civilian population from the guerrillas by forcing them to live in compounds. Villagers were forced to stay in the PVs by strict dusk-to-dawn curfews. Curfew-breakers were shot. Forced removals combined with the curfew meant that some people could not reach their fields to cultivate. In the first year of protected villages in one area, deaths increased by 37 per cent. Eighty per cent of these were from starvation and one in every five adults (let alone children, who were more vulnerable) suffered from malnutrition. Parallel with the PV policy was "Operation Turkey," the army's ironic code name for a policy of destroying food supplies in the rural areas. The ostensible aim was to allow only the barest minimum of food to reach the rural population so that they would have none to share with the guerrillas. The army burned down kraals and granaries, closed shops and grinding mills and shot cattle. The combined effect of the protected villages and Operation Turkey was to increase the demoralization and war weariness of the people and, arguably, to create pressure on the leaders of the nationalist parties to accept less favorable terms for independence than they might otherwise have held out for. At independence the outlying areas of Zimbabwe faced an acute food crisis as a direct result of these policies.*

The systematic torture and killing of suspected nationalist sympathizers by the security forces have been widely documented, principally by the Catholic Commission for Justice and Peace, a local organization which continues to monitor human rights issues in post-independence Zimbabwe. However, the following account, which gives a taste of the repression visited on rural Zimbabweans, comes from a recent book written by Bruce Moore-King,

---

* Richard Carver and David Sanders, "Why Soames will have to speed food to war zones," *Sunday Times*, London, December 23, 1979.

6

a former soldier in the Grey's Scouts, an elite counterinsurgency unit of the Rhodesian army:

> A man hangs spreadeagled, handcuffed to a steel bed-frame. ... The bed-frame is standing propped against the interior of the rondavel, almost vertical. The man is naked, handcuffs tight at each hand and each ankle, stretching him. His head is lolling, face gazing blindly down at his feet, but shortly the frame will be rotated and he will hang upside down.
>
> Around the ranch house a maze of trenches and barbed wire meanders, dotted with green canvas tents and heavily covered with ammunition pits. There are numerous mortar craters, the freshest having arrived the night before. The ranch manager and his wife have elected to stay, a show of deliberate defiance, and the man on the bed-frame is their boss boy, they've known him for nine years.
>
> There are three elements of the security forces present on the ranch, a company of territorials on call up, a platoon of police special constabulary — black men in blue overalls — under the command of an eighteen-year-old white policeman, and the troop of Grey's Scouts that have been helicoptered in because of the deteriorating situation on the ranch.
>
> There are two men in the rondavel with the prisoner, an SB [Special Branch] officer, and the commander of the Grey's troop. ... The man on the bed-frame groans, and the troop commander speaks: "Give us a hand." Together they rotate the bed-frame until the man is hanging upside-down. The troop commander, Kelly, picks up a length of thick, high-pressure compressor hose and hits the prisoner across the thighs and testicles with it. The prisoner screams.
>
> "I thought that would wake you up, you sonofabitch!"
>
> ... The man on the bed has a wire in his anus, and another attached to his testicles with a crocodile clip. Kelly is twisting the crank of an old telephone dynamo in short bursts. ...
>
> The security forces are getting nowhere and Kelly desperately needs some information to act on — ideally where the enemy are basing up. He is sure the senior boss boy knows.

The hands of the man on the bed are swollen like balloons, his face is not recognizably human. Kelly wraps one wire around the man's scrotum, attaches the crocodile clip on the other to his nipple. The interrogation goes on. Kelly is sweating and angry. A smelling-salts bottle is used to revive the man on the bed-frame. . . .

That night the man on the bed-frame talks, and in the morning the Grey's assault the position he has identified, but it is deserted. Only the fleeting remains of habitation show that it has been recently and regularly occupied. The man on the iron bed-frame has held out long enough.

Kelly orders a group of four volunteers to take the man into the bush and shoot him.

This they do.*

Independence

The two parties waging guerrilla war against the Rhodesian regime, Mugabe's ZANU and Nkomo's ZAPU, formed a Patriotic Front and took a common position in reaction to the various settlement proposals which were debated in international circles in the late 1970s. On the other hand the United African National Council of Bishop Abel Muzorewa, along with a faction of ZANU led by Reverend Ndabaningi Sithole, collaborated in an "internal settlement" in 1978. Muzorewa became Prime Minister but real power still rested with the white-controlled state structures. In late 1979 all parties attended a conference sponsored by Britain, the nominal colonial power, at Lancaster House in London. A constitution and formula for the transition to independence was agreed. In elections in March 1980 Mugabe's ZANU-PF gained an absolute majority of seats in Parliament, with ZAPU taking most of the remainder, apart from 20 per cent of seats reserved for the white electorate under the Lancaster House constitution. Zimbabwe became independent in April 1980 with Robert Mugabe as Prime Minister at the head of a coalition

---

*   Bruce Moore-King, *White Man, Black War*, Harare 1988, pp52-6.

government largely composed of ZANU-PF and ZAPU.* The new government embarked on an important series of reforms to extend social benefits such as health care and universal primary education to the whole population.

The government's watchword was "reconciliation" and Mugabe received wide international praise for his tolerance of the Rhodesian politicians and security personnel who had imprisoned him and killed so many of his supporters. Many of the worst human rights criminals fled the country at independence, often to find similar positions within the South African security apparatus. But other prominent Rhodesians associated with human rights abuse stayed on: Ian Smith himself, Law and Order Minister P K van der Byl, Lieutenant-General Peter Walls, whom Mugabe retained as army chief of staff, and Ken Flower, the head of the Central Intelligence Organization. The last-named, in an autobiography published shortly before his recent death, relates a conversation with Mugabe after being told that he was to be kept on as CIO director despite serious allegations by the Commissioner of Police that Flower had orchestrated attempts to assassinate Mugabe during the 1980 election campaign:

> He had no wish to talk of the allegations against me, dismissing the Commissioner as just another police informer and he laughed when I showed readiness to confirm some of our attempts to kill him.
>
> "Yes, but they all failed, otherwise we would not be here together," he remarked. "And do not expect me to applaud your failures."
>
> He paused for a moment and then continued: "As far as I have realized the position, we were trying to kill each other; that's what the war was about. What I am concerned with now is that

---

* Two important constitutional changes were enacted in 1987. The 20 white seats in the House of Assembly were abolished and replaced by non-constituency seats, for which the remainder of the House of Assembly formed an electoral college. Also an executive presidency was introduced - the post being taken by Mugabe. Hitherto Reverend Canaan Banana had been Zimbabwe's non-executive president.

my public statements should be believed when I say that I have drawn a line through the past. . . ."*

Just as important was the retention of lower ranking military and security officials who had been responsible for human rights abuse. A striking example was cited by Joseph Lelyveld:

> In Harare, I had asked Emmerson Munangagwa, the Cabinet minister who was regarded as Prime Minister Mugabe's most influential security adviser, about the reports that the white officers [accused of acts of sabotage against the Zimbabwean air force] and numerous blacks had been tortured. He responded elliptically, avoiding a categorical answer but seeking to impress on me his own sense of revulsion over any use of torture, which was rooted in his experiences as a "freedom fighter." The first thing he did, he said, when he took over his department was to revisit a room in a police station where he had been tortured by white officers who hung him upside down by leg irons from butcher's hooks that ran along a track on the ceiling. This enabled the interrogators, the Minister said, to bat his suspended body back and forth on the track from one end of the room to the other, as if he were the puck in an adaptation of hockey. The game continued until he lost consciousness. The day after the independence ceremonies, the butcher's hooks were still on the ceiling, and astonishingly, his former interrogators were now on his staff, as was another official who acknowledged having once sent him a letter bomb. They told him they had just been doing their jobs; he then promised they could start in independent Zimbabwe with a "clean slate." Some had later proved to be South African agents, but others still appeared to be loyal officers, the minister said. In the beginning he had no choice but to trust them, he explained. Zimbabwe could not be expected to dismantle its only security agency.**

---

*   Ken Flower, *Serving Secretly*, London 1987, pp1-3.

**   Joseph Lelyveld, *Move Your Shadow - South Africa, Black and White*, New York 1985, p213.

Bill Berkeley, who visited Zimbabwe for the Lawyers Committee for Human Rights, learned something similar when he interviewed Mnangagwa in 1985:

> He confirmed that a number of the CIO agents who tortured him are still working for the CIO, including one who entered the office during the interview to provide the Minister with statistics requested for this report. "Did you see that one," Munangagwa said. "He was one of the ones who tortured me." Asked if there were others in a similar position, the Minister replied, "There are many." Asked how he felt about the presence of such men in his agency, Munangagwa shrugged but said nothing.*

The reasons for retaining such people are probably twofold. One was the explanation which Mnangagwa gave to Lelyveld: Rhodesian officials had to stay, regardless of their crimes, because the well-being of the security apparatus depended on it. Even on purely pragmatic grounds such reasoning is highly questionable. In 1988 the government claimed to have uncovered a South African spy-ring centered on Kevin Woods, who until shortly beforehand had been a CIO official. This group was alleged to have been responsible for acts of sabotage leading to a number of deaths. The sabotage group will undoubtedly have been helped by their inside access to Zimbabwean intelligence.

The second reason for extending an olive branch to Rhodesian security officials was political. Mugabe was (and is) eager to avoid antagonizing the economically crucial white community. Although many whites have emigrated since independence, the farming community has generally stayed and benefited from an agricultural boom, while whites still occupy many important positions in commerce and business. The disastrous exodus of skills which has hampered neighboring Mozambique since Portuguese colonists fled at independence in 1975 has been successfully avoided. Many of the small white community were involved in the security forces at some level during the 1970s. The last thing that Mugabe wanted was the fear of a witch-hunt against whites.

---

*   Lawyers Committee for Human Rights, *Zimbabwe: Wages of War*, New York 1986, p42.

11

The threat to bring Ian Smith and his colleagues to trial — often uttered in the days of the independence struggle — seems to have been scarcely considered. Yet there would have been good moral grounds for doing so. Zimbabwean historian Lawrence Vambe was recently quoted as saying:

> We could have tried and hanged Mr Smith. We could have tried all those who participated in Smith's war who had blood on their hands. If there was a compulsion to settle old scores, this country would have seen much more suffering than we have seen, especially with the whites.*

All Ministers and government servants were indemnified under Rhodesian law for acts carried out in good faith in defence of national security. However, there is no indication that the new government ever considered the possibility of nullifying the indemnity legislation in order to prosecute the human rights violators, as happened, for example, in Argentina in 1983.** A prosecution would have sent a clear signal to the Zimbabwean security forces that human rights abuse would be met with the full force of the law. However, Mugabe was neither the first nor last leader to come to power in such circumstances and decide that the interests of national stability were best served by reconciliation rather than prosecution.

What is quite indefensible, however, is that officials known to be responsible for gross human rights abuses should not only not have been prosecuted but should have retained their positions in the security apparatus. There have been a number of reports of torture by former Rhodesian officials

---

* Quoted in Bill Berkeley, "One Party Fits All," *The New Republic*, March 6, 1989. Berkeley comments: "Some Zimbabweans cite that record as precedent for sweeping the more recent conflict under the rug."

** See Amnesty International, *Argentina: The Military Juntas and Human Rights*, London 1987. Zalaquett comments that if the junta's self-amnesty law, the "Law of National Pacification," had been "simply repealed, the fact that at one point in time it was in force would have produced the legal effect that the conducts it amnestied could not be made punishable again without violating the principle of non-retroactive application of criminal law. A law that is deemed null, instead, never produced any legal effects." (Jose Zalaquett, "Confronting human rights violations committed by former governments: principles applicable and political constraints," Aspen Institute for Humanistic Studies Conference on "State Crimes: Punishment or Pardon," November 1988.)

against alleged opponents of the Zimbabwean Government. For example, a senior ZAPU official, Pollant Jabavu Mpofu, described his torture in 1982 at the hands of Koroneli Nyathi, a former Rhodesian CIO official whose name crops up repeatedly in testimonies of torture:

> Koroneli called four of his staff who said they were going to give me special treatment and took me to a small dark room and told me to remove all of my clothing. They then left me locked in that room which was windowless and completely dark, for about 15 minutes. I remained naked and when they returned my hands were handcuffed behind my back....

> They then connected electrical equipment and commenced to subject my toes to electric shocks. I was crying out with pain while they continually demanded that I admit the charges. I continued to deny their charges saying if I knew nothing it was impossible for me to tell them what they wanted to.

> They then took the *gurok* [a sort of sack] full of salted water and tied it around my neck while continuing to administer electric shocks to me. By using the electric shocks they forced me to drink the salted water and when I was unable to drink more and my stomach was full they forced me, still handcuffed, to lie on the floor. One man then stood on my stomach and forced me to vomit the salted water. I vomited until I was vomiting blood.*

By no means all torture under the Mugabe government has been carried out by former Rhodesian officials. The more general point, however, is that the CIO and police were inherited intact and have survived more or less unchanged. There was never a purge of human rights abusers from these bodies — on the contrary the government seems proud of the fact that it bears no grudge against torturers. It is not surprising, then, that the culture of torture has survived into the post-independence era. One former Rhodesian police officer interviewed by Bill Berkeley makes the point:

---

*   Interview with Richard Carver, May 1984.

Nothing the police are doing now is new. The police have learned all their bad habits from the Rhodesian police. The beatings, the electric shock. . . .

I was a member of the Rhodesian police force. I know what went on. I became powerfully disillusioned by what I saw. You know, we were told we were fighting the battle for civilization and all, against barbarism.*

Crisis in Matabeleland

Electoral support for ZANU-PF and ZAPU in the 1980 election largely followed ethnic lines. All ZAPU's 20 seats came from Matabeleland, where the predominant ethnic group is the Ndebele, or from the ethnically mixed Midlands. ZANU-PF won no seats in Matabeleland and drew most of its support from the majority Shona speakers. The original split between ZANU and ZAPU in the 1960s had nothing to do with the Ndebele-Shona division, but a combination of political accident and conscious tribalism by some party leaders combined to make it a potent factor by the time of independence.

The conflict first blew up in the army. At independence it was agreed to integrate the ZANLA and ZIPRA** guerrillas into a single national army along with the former Rhodesian forces. If anything the former guerrillas were probably less prone to party or ethnic sectarianism than some of their political leaders. However, there was a widespread perception that the fighters who had made the greatest sacrifices for Zimbabwe's independence were having the least share in its benefits. Such frustration erupted into fighting between former ZANLA and ZIPRA guerrillas encamped at Entumbane township in Bulawayo awaiting integration. Initial fighting in November 1980 died down after a few days. A second outburst in February 1981 spread to other groups of guerrillas awaiting integration and was only ended when the government deployed ex-Rhodesian units and the air force against former ZIPRA personnel, killing more

---

*   Lawyers Committee, *op cit*, p90-1.

**   The Zimbabwe African National Liberation Army (ZANLA) was the military wing of
         ZANU; the Zimbabwe People's Liberation Army (ZIPRA) was its ZAPU counterpart.

14

than 100. This action prompted many ex-ZIPRA members to desert and go back to the bush with their guns. These desertions accelerated a year later when the government announced that it had uncovered arms caches on ZAPU-owned properties. Joshua Nkomo and other ZAPU Ministers were sacked from the government and former ZIPRA leaders, notably Dumiso Dabengwa and Lookout Masuku, the deputy army commander, were arrested and charged with treason. They were later acquitted, but rearrested and detained without charge until 1986.*

From early 1982 a military Task Force led by Lieutenant-Colonel Lionel Dyke, a former Rhodesian officer, was deployed in Matabeleland North against the ex-ZIPRA "dissidents," as the government called them. There were frequent reports of detention and torture of villagers. One eyewitness from Tsholotsho is reported as describing what happened when the Task Force came to his village:

> The soldiers beat and hit us and threatened us in a terrible way. They accused us of feeding dissidents. They hit one old woman and said that she was a mother of dissidents.
>
> Then the White soldier picked one boy and asked him what he was going to say. He said he knew nothing to say about dissidents. The White soldier took his gun from his belt and just shot the boy in the head. Just in front of us.**

In January 1983 the Task Force was replaced by the Fifth Brigade, a unit which had been specially trained by North Korean military advisers and which was outside the normal command structure of the army, being directly under the control of the Prime Minister's office. The brigade appeared to be

---

*   Incidentally, the case of Dabengwa and Masuku also illustrates the folly of retaining former Rhodesian CIO officers. The ex-ZIPRA army officer who carried out the caching of arms appears to have been a police agent working under the orders of Matt Calloway, the head of CIO in Hwange. Calloway later defected to South Africa where he became a crucial figure in organizing support for the "dissidents". The continued detention of the two popular ZIPRA leaders was an important factor provoking anti-government sentiment in Matabeleland. Calloway's role is outlined in Joseph Hanlon, "Destabilisation and the Battle to Reduce Dependence" in Colin Stoneman (ed), *Zimbabwe's Prospects*, London 1988.

**   "Rhodesian troops prop up Mugabe," *Africa Now*, July 1984.

almost exclusively composed of Shona-speaking ex-ZANLA combatants. In the weeks that followed, the Fifth Brigade carried out many killings of villagers in Matabeleland North. Reports indicated that often they visited villages with lists of ZAPU officials and sympathizers, who were singled out and killed. They made little attempt to engage the "dissidents" militarily. There was an ugly strand of tribalism in the behavior of the Fifth Brigade: the Ndebele were being punished for crimes their ancestors were supposed to have committed against the Shona. Finally, in mid-1983, Mugabe responded to international pressure and withdrew the Fifth Brigade from Matabeleland. A Commission of Inquiry was set up to investigate allegations of army abuses; although it submitted a report to the government, its findings were never made public.

However, at the beginning of 1984 the Fifth Brigade was redeployed in Matabeleland South and the pattern of abuse was repeated. Again there were reports of army killings and torture at a number of *ad hoc* army camps: Belaghwe, Sun Yet Sen and Mphoengs. But this time there was also a strict dusk-to-dawn curfew and restrictions on the movement of food into the area. This was at the height of a severe drought which affected the whole of Zimbabwe, but Matabeleland South worst of all. There had been some attempt to restrict food supplies in Matabeleland North in 1983 but now Operation Turkey was being wholeheartedly revived. Again there was an international outcry and the Fifth Brigade was withdrawn. The journalist who played the greatest role in exposing the killings, Peter Godwin of the London *Sunday Times*, was expelled from the country. (Nick Worrall of *The Guardian* had been expelled the previous year.)

Exactly how many people died at the hands of the Fifth Brigade will never be known. The Justice and Peace Commission stated in 1983 that it had gathered firm evidence of 469 civilian killings "for the most part by government soldiers." Clearly the actual death toll was much higher — 1500 would be a conservative estimate.

In only a tiny handful of cases were security force members brought to justice for these killings. One exceptional case was the sentence of death imposed on four Fifth Brigade soldiers for killings in February 1983 — but in this instance the victims including an off-duty army officer, Lieutenant Edias

Ndlovu. In June 1988 the four soldiers were among 75 members of the security forces released under an amnesty.*

The initial "dissidents" were from the left wing of ZIPRA and had historically maintained strong links with the African National Congress of South Africa (ANC). But the South African Government saw the instability in Matabeleland as a chance to pursue its own ends by arming and sponsoring its own "dissident" bands. While the security forces were carrying out their abuses, the "dissidents" were committing their own atrocities against the civilian population and, on occasions, against others such as tourists and missionaries. One of the incidents which grabbed international attention occurred in November 1987 when "dissidents" hacked to death 16 members of a Protestant mission at Esigodini, including babies and small children. It was such brutality that affected the hapless people of Matabeleland for six years or so.

However, in certain instances there is evidence to suggest that killings were carried out not by "dissidents" but by "pseudo-gangs" of the security forces. The tactic of impersonating guerrillas while committing atrocities was widely used by the Rhodesian forces in the independence war. In November 1985 Luke and Jean Kumalo, a Methodist headmaster and his wife, were killed at Thekwane school in Matabeleland South. The official version was that dissidents were responsible. However, there were a number of unanswered questions. Why did soldiers at an army camp three kilometers away not intervene, when the attackers were at the school for several hours, firing shots and burning buildings? The army did not even arrive when the school staff sent for help after the attackers had left. Why were the attackers wearing military uniform? And why did they leave a note saying that Luke and Jean Kumalo were being killed for passing information to Amnesty International? In response to Amnesty International's call for an inquiry into the killings, the government stated that it had captured a member of the "dissident" band responsible. However, as far as Africa Watch can tell, no one has been charged with the murders.

---

*   See below.

17

In early 1985 a new pattern of human rights abuse emerged. Dozens — possibly hundreds — of people throughout Matabeleland and Midlands "disappeared" as a result of nighttime abductions by armed men. The government's explanation was that the "disappeared" people had gone to join the "dissidents" but there are a number of factors suggesting that the security forces were in fact responsible. The victims were often middle-aged or old men — not the young men who might be expected to join the "dissidents." They were often driven away in vehicles — yet there are no recorded instances of "dissidents" having vehicles. On occasions vehicles were identified as belonging to the security forces and sometimes the tracks were followed to local military camps. The armed men who came often spoke only poor Ndebele — the "dissidents" were usually fluent Ndebele speakers.* None of those abducted has reappeared since the "dissidents" were amnestied and came out of the bush in May 1988.

Throughout this period ZAPU members, especially former ZIPRA combatants, were being detained under the same Emergency Powers used against them by the Rhodesian Government, and often tortured. After general elections in mid-1985, which ZANU-PF again won convincingly, there was a further clampdown on ZAPU, with hundreds of its members detained on the allegation that they were helping the "dissidents."

There is ample testimony on the use of torture by the CIO and by a special police unit: PISI (Police Internal Security and Intelligence). *Pisi* is the Sindebele word for hyena. A common method was to submerge the victim's head in a canvas bag of water until he or she lost consciousness. This would be repeated frequently. Beatings were systematic, often to the soles of the feet with rubber truncheons, *sjamboks* (rawhide whips) or weighted hosepipes. Electric shocks were also used. In some cases people died under torture: *post mortem* examinations and inquests provide an important source of evidence. An inquest found that Francis Sibanda, 30, died in July 1983 from a subdural haematoma and compression of the brain sustained during his detention at Stops Camp, a police and CIO holding center in Bulawayo. Sindiso Ndlovu, 25, died in July

---

*   See below.

1984 of multiple injuries caused by beating with a stick, according to the *post mortem* report. An inquest recorded a verdict of "death due to injuries sustained in an assault." At the time of his death he was detained at Stops Camp; a police witness told the inquest that Ndlovu was uninjured when he was arrested. Temba Moyo died in August 1984 in hospital in Bulawayo after being admitted there from custody in Stops Camp. The *post mortem* report states that the cause of death was "acute renal failure due to assault." It describes a total of 17 bruises caused "by either a stick or rope of length not less than 16 cm and width about 1.2 cm."

In late 1985 Amnesty International publicly stated its concern over torture in Zimbabwe. It followed this with a memorandum to the government detailing 21 cases of torture and seeking an impartial investigation. A report by the Lawyers Committee for Human Rights in May 1986 provided a more comprehensive review of the human rights situation. As with the expulsion of journalists who reported the Matabeleland killings, the government response was to blame the bearer of bad news. All allegations of torture were categorically denied. Amnesty International, which had adopted many members of the government as "prisoners of conscience" during their long spells in Rhodesian jails, was denounced as an "enemy of Zimbabwe." Former prisoner of conscience Robert Mugabe described it as "Amnesty Lies International," while Home Affairs Minister Enos Nkala (another Amnesty International alumnus) threatened to detain anyone who provided the organization with information.

Even so, the government appears to have taken Amnesty International's allegations seriously. Enos Nkala, who was the most vocal in denouncing Amnesty International, also visited Stops Camp to try to establish the truth of the allegations. Strict instructions were disseminated throughout the police force forbidding torture. The result has been a considerable improvement in police behavior. On the other hand the CIO appears not to have modified its treatment of prisoners.* At the same time, many of the ZAPU political detainees were released. Partly this too was a response to international

---

* For evidence of continuing torture, see Chapter 5.

criticism of Zimbabwe's human rights record, but much of the impulse for the releases came from a new atmosphere of political reconciliation. In December 1987 ZANU-PF and ZAPU signed an agreement to unify the two parties. This was widely seen at the time as the establishment of a *de facto* one-party state, preparing the way for 1990, by which time there would be no constitutional impediment to establishing one *de jure*.* Subsequent developments may have led to a reconsideration of the objective of a one-party system, though the unification of ZANU-PF is proceeding and has brought a peaceful political solution to the Matabeleland problem.

---

* The preservation of a multiparty system was entrenched in the Lancaster House constitution. Until 1990 it can only be overturned by a 100 percent vote in both chambers of parliament.

3. AMNESTY

The December 1987 unity agreement was followed by a Cabinet reshuffle which brought ZAPU Ministers back into the government for the first time since 1982, but also removed the hardline anti-ZAPU Enos Nkala from the Ministry of Home Affairs and replaced him with Moven Mahachi. Soon after his appointment Mahachi set about releasing the remaining Emergency Powers detainees. By April 1988 only a handful remained, who were released to mark the eighth anniversary of independence. Also on independence day Mugabe announced an amnesty for all those "dissidents" still in the bush who surrendered by the end of May. Some 113 did so and Matabeleland's security problems were largely at an end. Under the terms of the amnesty none of those who surrendered could be prosecuted for crimes committed while they were in the bush. There was considerable popular discontent when "Gayigusu" — Morgan Sango Nkomo — took advantage of the amnesty. He had been responsible for the November 1987 massacre of missionaries at Esigodini and other atrocities.

In June 1988 the government announced that 75 members of the security forces or ZANU-PF sentenced or awaiting trial for human rights violations were also to be released as a "special category" under the amnesty. Among those released was Robert Masikini, a CIO official who had been sentenced to death only a week earlier for the murder of Paul Mlotshwa, a political detainee in his custody.

Also released were the four Fifth Brigade soldiers, Charles Simango, Samuel Chayana, George Chihwayi and Julius Gwatirera, sentenced to death for the murder of Lieutenant Edias Ndlovu and three others in February 1983. The four were picked up by the army from a petrol station on the Victoria Falls to Bulawayo road. According to the inquest, "the deceased were tied with pieces of fibre, were got down on the ground and repeatedly stabbed with bayonets, much as a hunter slaughtering a wounded animal with a spear." Lieutenant

21

Ndlovu died from a bayonet wound of the liver, his wife Jennifer Khumalo from a bayonet wound of the heart. Their companions were not identified by the inquest. The man died from a bayonet wound to the frontal lobe of the brain and the woman from being shot in the chest. They were later named as Modern Smart Moyo and Anna Chipo Masuku. A Supreme Court judge, dismissing the four soldiers' appeal in April 1987, commented:

> What was established was that the appellants abducted the four unfortunate and innocent deceased from the petrol station and, after subjecting them to torture — and the two females to some degrading form of sexual abuse — they slaughtered them in a most atrocious, cruel and cold-blooded manner.

It is clearly to the government's credit that members of the security forces such as Robert Masikini and the four Fifth Brigade soldiers should have been brought to justice. It is also to the credit of those who testified against them, in the Masikini case despite threats from the CIO. Not only has Masikini now been released but he is reported to be working again for the CIO.

The government has attempted to justify this amnesty on the grounds of political balance. Certainly much public opinion was outraged that the likes of Gayigusu were to escape prosecution. Government officials have argued to Africa Watch that security force members had to be amnestied in a parallel move to assuage discontent in the ranks of the armed forces and ZANU-PF.

However, the parallel is a false one. Not only had Masikini and the Fifth Brigade soldiers been found guilty in a court of law, whereas Gayigusu had not; more importantly the former were government servants with a responsibility for protecting the human rights of Zimbabweans. When human rights abusers are allowed to escape punishment, this has a significance which goes beyond their individual case. It sends a signal to members of the security forces that in practice they are immune to punishment for the human rights violations they commit.

At independence the Zimbabwean Government inherited the Indemnity and Compensation Act, which indemnified all government servants for acts carried out in defence of national security. In other words it precluded the possibility of prosecution for torture, arbitrary arrest or unlawful killing. Within a year of independence a senior Government Minister and secretary general of ZANU-PF, Edgar Tekere, had successfully invoked the Indemnity and Compensation Act to avoid conviction on a charge of murdering a white farmer in August 1980. After the Tekere case the government bowed to political pressure and repealed the Indemnity and Compensation Act. However, it was quietly replaced by the Emergency Powers (Security Forces Indemnity) Regulations, which had a similar effect. The Minister of Home Affairs had the power to issue a certificate disallowing any civil or criminal proceedings against state officials acting "in good faith" for the protection of state security. In 1984 these regulations were tested in court when a Harare attorney, Denis Rhodes Granger, sued the Minister of State for Security for unlawful arrest by the CIO. The Supreme Court unanimously held that the "good faith" provision was unconstitutional; the official's motives had to be objectively tested in a court of law. The Granger judgment was not widely publicized in the government-controlled press — so it is unlikely that it had much immediate effect on the behavior of the security forces — but it did oblige the government to repeal the Emergency Powers (Security Forces Indemnity) Regulations.*

In May 1989 the House of Assembly passed a Bill indemnifying National Park game wardens for acts carried out in the course of their anti-poaching activities. In recent months a number of poachers, mainly Zambian nationals, have been killed by Zimbabwean game wardens as a result of an apparent "shoot-to-kill" policy.

The June 1988 amnesty for security force members was an escape route for those human rights violators who did not benefit from the indemnity provisions. Not only does the amnesty mean that human rights violators are not punished; it also signals that the government does not regard such crimes as sufficiently serious to warrant punishment; and it removes from citizens any possibility of redress for crimes committed against them by government servants. This violates Article 8 of the Universal Declaration of Human Rights, which states:

---

*   This is a good illustration of the importance of the justiciable Declaration of Rights introduced in the independence constitution. Rhodesia had no such bill of rights.

Everyone has the right to an effective remedy by the competent national tribunals for acts violating the fundamental rights granted him by the constitution or by law.*

One of the most important remedies for violation of rights is the payment of damages. On this Zimbabwe has a poor record. The Emergency Powers (Security Forces Indemnity) Regulations were introduced after a High Court judgment in 1982 in favor of a Member of Parliament, Wally Stuttaford, who had been detained and tortured. He had been kicked and punched, made to do strenuous physical exercise (he was aged over 60), and had his hair pulled. Pencils were inserted between his fingers and his hands were squeezed. Evidence of his ill-treatment was established by a medical examination. Stuttaford brought a civil action for damages against the government. The authorities ordered that the action be heard *in camera* and that the outcome should not be disclosed. In fact Stuttaford was successful and received a substantial award. He has not received a cent. Africa Watch knows of no case in which the Zimbabwean authorities have paid damages to victims of human rights abuse. The case of Member of Parliament Kembo Mohadi, who was awarded damages for torture in 1986, has already been mentioned. Similarly Denis Granger, who brought the test case which led to the repeal of the Security Forces Indemnity Regulations, was awarded damages which he never received.

In 1986 Mugabe was questioned in Parliament about the government's failure to pay damages awarded against it for unlawful arrest and detention. He replied:

---

* Article 2(3) of the International Covenant on Civil and Political Rights (which Zimbabwe has not signed or ratified) amplifies the point:
Each State Party to the present Covenant undertakes:
(a) To ensure that any person whose rights or freedoms as herein recognized are violated shall have an effective remedy, notwithstanding that the violation has been committed by persons acting in an official capacity;
(b) To ensure that any person claiming such a remedy shall have his right thereto determined by competent judicial, administrative or legislative authorities, or by any other competent authority provided for by the legal system of the State, and to develop the possibilities of judicial remedy;
(c) To ensure that the competent authorities shall enforce such remedies when granted.

If Government — and I want to say this as a matter of principle — were to be awarding damages and paying huge sums of money that are involved in these cases, some of which are of a petty nature, Government would in my view be using the taxpayers' money wrongfully. It is true that Government has not paid damages. Where, for example, a person suffers injury as a result of an accident involving on the one side, a vehicle driven by a Government employee, we have paid — we have not refused. However, where people take advantage of our liberal situation to go to court and win on technicalities, they should not expect that Government is going to use the people's resources to enrich them when we believe in some cases that they are wrongdoers.*

It had apparently not occurred to the Prime Minister that the misuse of taxpayers' money came with the initial unlawful arrest, not the subsequent award of damages to the wronged parties. There is no legal remedy in Zimbabwe if the State refuses to pay damages awarded by the court.**

As has been described, government officials have justified the amnesty of security force officials by stating that it was parallel with the amnesty for "dissidents." In fact the "dissidents" who benefited from the amnesty had not been charged with any offence, whereas most of the security forces personnel were serving court-imposed sentences. The individuals whose situation most closely paralleled the security force members were more than 200 people serving prison sentences for "dissident-related" offenses. Apparently some of these prisoners have been held since as long ago as 1982. Many received trials in magistrates' courts at which they were not legally represented. In at least one case where the accused did receive legal representation — that of Alibaba Dlodlo, Samson Nhari, Frank Nyoni and Amos Moyo, convicted after an attack on the Prime Minister's residence in 1982 — there has been widespread doubt about the verdict. These prisoners are serving sentences for offenses ranging

---

*   Speech of July 16, 1986, cited in G Feltoe, *A Guide to Zimbabwean Cases Relating to Security, Emergency Powers and Unlawful Arrest and Detention*, Legal Resources Foundation, Harare 1988, pp8.

**   *Ibid*, pp8-9.

from failing to report the presence of "dissidents" to murder. Without exception they are ZAPU supporters or come from Matabeleland or Midlands provinces. In ZAPU circles and in Matabeleland there is resentment at the discriminatory treatment compared with convicted security force members. But there is also disquiet at the discrimination between different categories of "dissidents." Those who evaded capture until April 1988 are immune from prosecution, whereas anyone arrested before that date cannot benefit from the amnesty. (Needless to say, the same distinction does not apply in the security force cases.) In April 1989 Africa Watch asked the Minister of Justice, Emmerson Mnangagwa, why these prisoners had not benefited from the amnesty. He stated that their cases were being reviewed on an individual basis and that some 75 had already been released (a claim which human rights bodies in Harare and Bulawayo were unable to confirm). Government officials have claimed that no one is still serving a sentence for failing to report or aiding "dissidents." Again this cannot be confirmed. However, even if true, this does not answer the basic imbalance between convicted security officials who have received a blanket amnesty and convicted government opponents whose cases must be reviewed individually.

"Disappearances"

Another group of people who have so far failed to receive redress are the relatives of those who "disappeared" in Matabeleland and Midlands. No one seriously entertains any hope that the "disappeared" will now return. But, apart from the emotional need for their families to have their fate explained, there is also an important practical problem. Until the "disappeared" are officially declared to be dead, their families do not have any right to their assets. Many of the families have no income and are virtually destitute. They are also unable to claim any compensation from the state.

The relatives' hopes for a legal remedy have been kept alive in a suit filed by nine women from the Silobela communal land of Midlands Province, seeking an official explanation of the whereabouts of their husbands or brothers, abducted by armed men on the night of January 30, 1985. All those who "disappeared" were Ndebeles and ZAPU supporters, although Silobela is mixed between Ndebeles and Shonas, ZAPU and ZANU-PF supporters. In mid-1984 an off-duty policeman named Maphosa was killed in the area. "Dissidents" were said to be responsible and the ZANU-PF youth wing beat up many people, including Patrick Mthethwa and Enoch Tshuma, who later "disappeared," and Winnie Mabhikwa whose husband Dennis was another of the nine. Enoch Tshuma was hospitalized by the beating and nearly lost an eye. According to an affidavit by Patrick Mthethwa's wife Lucy, the ZANU-PF District Chairman, Samuel Chivange, who is also a leader of the People's Militia, threatened: "You people of Silobela have killed my cousin. Now we have evil spirits which will steal people at night." Other women also recalled Chivange's threats.

On the night of January 30 armed men came to the area. They knocked on the doors of the nine families, identifying themselves as people who "lived in the bush." Lucy Mthethwa commented:

> I have never seen dissidents before but we are always told that dissidents are Ndebeles. However, these people were certainly not Ndebeles and they spoke in broken Sindebele. Furthermore, from their appearance, they did not look like people who stayed in the bush. All this made me suspicious that they were in fact Government people.

The other women also remarked on the fact that they did not look like people from the bush and were not native Sindebele-speakers. The men were taken away. Sonile Dube followed her husband Simon and his abductors for a short distance:

> ... after a short while, I heard my husband crying out from the road. He was obviously in great pain as he shouted very loud. This went on for sometime.

> ... Eventually, the crying stopped. I then woke up our children and sat outside near our fence. After sometime, we heard vehicles passing by on the main road travelling towards Crossroads. There were three vehicles and they had their back lights flashing.

> ... The security forces in our area have small Nissan trucks and when these vehicles are gaining speed their engines have high pitched sounds which are recognizable. The three vehicles I heard on that night had that same high pitched sound.

Other women also said that they recognized the sound of the vehicles as being from security force Nissans. Lucy Mthethwa followed the footprints of her husband and the armed men: "They led to the marks of car tires near to the dip on the Loreto Road. There were lots of marks around that spot. There was also blood on the ground and sticks which had presumably been used for beating."

The abductions were reported to the police, but there were no follow-up operations by the security forces. Sonile Dube said in her affidavit:

> There were no patrols by the army or police and no question-ing of people. This was in stark contrast to the activities of the security forces after the death of Maphosa. This made me very suspicious.

A number of the women also commented that it was odd that this major event in the life of the area was never mentioned at ZANU-PF party meetings. All the women were convinced that their menfolk had been abducted by the security forces. Winnie Mabhikwa states that one member of ZANU-PF told her that Dennis was taken by the CIO.*

The nine women's suit was filed in the High Court in 1986 by a lawyer hired by the Roman Catholic Commission for Justice and Peace in Zimbabwe. The court ordered a police investigation into the case, which reported back, after much delay, in early 1989. However, the investigation did not go beyond the original affidavits by the wives. It was deficient in three particular areas. First, the police had failed to interview all relevant witnesses. For example, one man, David Mpofu from Commeryn Ranch, had sworn an affidavit saying that on the night of January 30 he saw his nephew, a special constable, driving towards the area where the abductions took place. He was not interviewed. Second, the police had not interviewed local ZANU-PF officials, notably Samuel Chivange, who had issued threats against local people. Third, the police did not investigate the use of police and security force vehicles on the night in question. The case still seems far from a satisfactory conclusion.

---

*   Affidavits sworn by Elida Jackson Mthambo Tshuma, Sonile Dube, Winnie Mabhikwa and Lucy Mthethwa, Harare, December 20, 1985.

In another case, court action has been more successful. The wife of Fraser Gibson Sibanda succeeded earlier this year in obtaining an admission that the police were responsible for her husband's unlawful killing. He had been arrested by police during a church service in Bulawayo on November 3, 1985. The reason for his arrest was apparently that he was wearing a badge depicting ZAPU leader Joshua Nkomo. His wife made inquiries at a number of different police stations in Bulawayo and was told that he was in the custody of PISI. He has not been seen again. There is the possibility of a criminal prosecution against the officer alleged to be responsible. In theory it is also possible for her to sue the police for damages. Whether she would ever receive any money is another matter.

The decision in the Fraser Sibanda case is important, since there is a series of similar "disappearances," involving not nighttime abductions by unidentified death squads, but prisoners who vanish after being arrested by the police or CIO. The following are some of the cases reported to Africa Watch:

Charles Mwase was arrested by the CIO on the morning of March 13, 1984 at his office in Edgars department store in Bulawayo, where he worked as a screenprinter. He is a demobilized former ZIPRA guerrilla, aged about 27 at the time of his arrest. He is reported to have been beaten at the time of his arrest and later taken to Gwanda, in Matabeleland South. This was during the period of the curfew in Matabeleland South during which there were many killings by the security forces. Charles Mwase has not been seen since.

Oscar Ncube was arrested in Tsholotsho, Matabeleland North, on February 6, 1985, and taken away in an army vehicle. His wife was later informed that he had been detained by the CIO at Stops Camp until September 10, 1985. In January 1986 the CIO told the Tsholotsho District Commissioner that Ncube had been handed over to the Criminal Investigation Department (CID) of the police in late 1985 and released. The CID denies this. The police in Tsholotsho have a different story altogether. They maintain that he was kidnapped by "dissidents" on February 2, 1985, four days before his arrest. Ncube has not been seen since.

Edward Moyo, who had previously given evidence to the Commission of Inquiry into army abuses in Matabeleland North, was arrested in Tsholotsho in July 1985. A few days later his brother, **Shadreck Denga Moyo**, was told to report to the CIO at Mabutweni police station in Bulawayo. He did so and neither brother has been seen since.

In none of these cases have the authorities provided any explanation for the "disappearance," nor, apparently, have they carried out any investigation. The Fraser Sibanda case shows that there may be some possibility of pursuing these "disappearances" through the courts, but it is the government's responsibility to initiate its own inquiries and to offer redress to the families of those prisoners found to have died. This obligation is particularly compelling in cases such as those cited above, in which the person "disappeared" after being taken into custody. The government and even some ZAPU leaders may be inclined to forget such cases as being past history, but for the families of the "disappeared," who have lost loved ones and often breadwinners, the absence is no less acute because the party leaders have signed a unity accord. The government should investigate the "disappearances" fully and bring to justice those officials found responsible for prolonged unlawful detention, torture or killing of prisoners.

4. STATE OF EMERGENCY AND ADMINISTRATION OF JUSTICE

Zimbabwe has been governed under a continuous state of emergency for nearly a quarter of a century. Since independence the constitution has required that parliament vote on renewing the emergency every six months. Since the government has a clear majority this vote has always been a formality, but the need for parliamentary approval has obliged the government to explain regularly why the emergency should be renewed. On each occasion the justification has been the constant threat from South Africa to Zimbabwe's stability, whether by its own direct activities, through the Matabeleland "dissidents," or now through RENAMO attacks in eastern Zimbabwe. These have all been genuine security problems: the "dissident" problem has already been referred to and the situation in eastern Zimbabwe is discussed in Chapter 6 below. South Africa itself has carried out bombings, political assassinations and military raids on its northern neighbor. Political strategists in Pretoria clearly perceive the danger to them of a successful multiracial Zimbabwe and have used a variety of tactics to try to sabotage the country's development. Arguably the continuing state of emergency in itself represents a triumph for Pretoria's strategy.

The Zimbabwean Government has not tried to refine its use of the state of emergency, for example by restricting its use to particular parts of the country. In January 1989, when Home Affairs Minister Moven Mahachi proposed to parliament the renewal of the state of emergency, he rested his argument almost exclusively on the situation in eastern Zimbabwe. Yet at the time he was speaking, none of those detained indefinitely under emergency powers had any connection with RENAMO or the eastern border. Since the renewal of the state of emergency a law lecturer has been detained and a number of opposition politicians, again none of them connected with RENAMO.

The Emergency Powers (Maintenance of Law and Order) Regulations, which give the authorities the power to detain without trial, are the main

31

reason why the state of emergency remains in force. The principal victims of detention without trial have been officials and supporters of ZAPU, including members of parliament. On a number of occasions detention powers have been invoked when the state has failed to secure a conviction in court. The powers are the same in all essentials as those enjoyed by the Rhodesian Government and used extensively against the nationalist movement. Although the numbers detained are far fewer now than in pre-independence days or in the mid-1980s, when hundreds were held under emergency powers, some cases still give cause for concern. Since detention without trial has been extensively abused, there must always be the fear of a return to the use of mass detentions in response to political opposition or declining security in the east of the country.

Individuals may be detained without charge under three different sections of the Emergency Powers (Maintenance of law and Order) Regulations:

- Section 17 empowers the Minister of Home Affairs to order the indefinite detention without trial of any individual if he considers this to be "expedient in the interests of public safety or public order."

- Section 21 empowers the police or security officials (such as the CIO) to detain anyone for up to 30 days if they believe that there are grounds which would justify a Ministerial detention order under Section 17.

- Section 53 empowers the police to detain anyone for up to 30 days for purposes of investigation.

The regulations require that a detainee be allowed to communicate with a lawyer immediately upon detention and that he or she should be served with written reasons for detention within seven days. In practice these requirements are often not complied with. Equally many detainees are held for longer than the prescribed 30-day period under Section 21 or Section 53 orders; lawyers are reluctant to challenge such illegal detentions in court for fear that their client might be detained under Section 17, under which there is no time limit.

The principal safeguard for anyone detained under Section 17 is the Detainees' Review Tribunal, composed of government-appointed lawyers. The tribunal must review all detainees' cases within 30 days of their being issued with a Section 17 order and every six months thereafter. In practice there is often a delay of several months before the first hearing. The tribunal sits *in camera* and it is an offence to reveal its proceedings. It reaches its decision on the balance of probabilities, rather than requiring the detaining authority to prove its case beyond reasonable doubt as it would have to in a criminal case. In practice this means that the burden shifts to the detainee to disprove the state's grounds for detention.* This led to a recent Supreme Court judgment laying down what constitutes adequate grounds for detention. The detainee must be informed of the essential facts which form the basis for detention. Reasons given must be sufficient to allow the detainee to make meaningful representations to the Review Tribunal.**

Although there have been a number of court cases in recent years challenging various technical deficiencies in the detention process, a detainee has no opportunity to challenge the *grounds* for detention in open court. A government-appointed tribunal which sits *in camera* clearly does not provide most of the internationally-accepted guarantees of a fair trial. Nevertheless, probably a majority of detainees are released on their first tribunal recommendation, suggesting that the authorities usually do not have good grounds for detaining in the first place.

---

*   Commenting on *Evans and Another v Chairman of the Review Tribunal and Another* HH-131-86, Feltoe writes:

   This case lays down that it is incumbent upon the Minister of Home Affairs to justify the detention. The degree of proof required is the same as that in a civil case, namely proof on a balance of probabilities. (However, the Supreme Court said that because personal liability is involved when it comes to detention, the degree of probability required is high...)

   The effect of this is that the person representing the Minister at review hearings is obliged to lead sufficient evidence against the detainee so as to prove the case against him on a balance of probabilities. Having heard both the State and the detainee's cases, the Tribunal is obliged to decide whether the case against the detainee has been proved on a balance of probabilities. If it has not, it must recommend release. (But even if the case has been proven on a balance of probabilities, it still remains for the Tribunal to decide whether on the facts proven against the detainee there is a justifiable basis for him to continue to be kept in detention.)

   (G Feltoe, *A Guide to Zimbabwean Cases relating to Security, Emergency Powers and Unlawful Arrest and Detention*, Legal Resources Foundation, Harare 1988, p7.)

**   *Minister of Home Affairs & Another v Austin & Another* S-79-86.

However, a worrying development recently has been the increasing readiness of the government to overrule Review Tribunal decisions. The tribunal's recommendations are purely advisory, but if the President decides not to comply, a notice to that effect must appear in the official *Gazette*. Before 1985 the government always complied with tribunal recommendations. In 1985 one *Gazette* notice appeared overruling a Review Tribunal decision and another in 1986. Since then there has been a rash of such notices. Despite all the formal limits on its powers and discretion, Review Tribunal members appear to have taken seriously their responsibility as an impartial arbiter between detainee and detaining authority. The government has been unhappy with the result and now takes little notice of what the tribunal says. A number of current detention cases illustrate the point.

John Lewis-Walker, a senior civil servant, was one of a group of six people arrested in September 1987 and detained at Chikurubi Maximum Security Prison, Harare, under the Emergency Powers (Maintenance of Law and Order) Regulations. The allegation against all of them was that they had spied for South Africa. The Review Tribunal recommended Lewis-Walker's release in early 1988, but the President overruled this. The six were then charged with espionage, although this charge was withdrawn in August 1988 and they were issued with new Section 17 detention orders. For a second time the Review Tribunal recommended Lewis-Walker's release and again this recommendation was overruled. Africa Watch understands that since then a further favorable tribunal decision has been overruled. Lewis-Walker was finally released in August 1989.

Patricia Brown, is one of the same group of six with Lewis-Walker and the outlines of her case are the same, with at least two favorable Review Tribunal recommendations disregarded. She was reported to be in a poor mental state as a consequence of her detention. She was finally released at the same time as John Lewis-Walker in August 1989.

Joseph Mujakati, aged 19 or 20, was arrested in January 1988. He is the nephew of Philip Conjwayo, who was convicted of murder by the High Court for his part in a bombing in Trenance, Bulawayo, on behalf of the South African Government. It is believed that the allegation against Mujakati is that he acted as a courier for his uncle. However, the Review Tribunal has recommended his release and Africa Watch is concerned that the only reason for his continuing detention is his family relationship to Conjwayo.

Terence and Gail Downey were arrested in July 1988, apparently on the allegation that they were involved in a plan to rescue Gail Downey's brother, Michael Smith, from Chikurubi where he was remanded on charges arising from the Trenance bombing and other alleged acts of violence on behalf of South Africa. However, we understand that the Review Tribunal subsequently recommended their release, although the government delayed for several months before acting on this recommendation in August 1989.

Leslie Johannes Lesia, a South African trader, was arrested in Mozambique in April or May 1987 and handed over, apparently without legal basis, to the Zimbabwean authorities. Lesia is alleged to have been so badly beaten by the CIO at Goromonzi detention center that both his legs were broken. Charges against him in connection with a bomb explosion in Harare in May 1987 were dropped in October 1988, but he remains in detention under emergency powers. By April 1989 the Review Tribunal had not yet considered his case. Thus Lesia had been imprisoned for two years without the grounds for his imprisonment having been reviewed by a competent tribunal, whether judicial or administrative.

Within Zimbabwe all these cases are politically sensitive because of the detainees' alleged connections with South Africa. But it is not enough to smear an individual by claiming that he or she has links with the South African security apparatus; the threat to Zimbabwe's "public safety or public order" must be proved to the satisfaction of the Review Tribunal. Africa Watch wrote to Home Affairs Minister Mahachi in May 1989, urging him to release these detainees. The letter concluded:

> We should stress that in none of these cases does Africa Watch seek to condone acts of sabotage or espionage, nor to minimize the very real threat to Zimbabwe's security posed by the South African Government and military apparatus. However, in each of these cases the detaining authority has not convinced an administrative tribunal sitting *in camera* that there

are sufficient grounds to deprive the individual concerned of his or her liberty.*

Judicial independence

One of the most disturbing aspects of detention without trial in Zimbabwe has been the re-detention of individuals acquitted by the courts. An early instance of this occurred in 1983 when the High Court acquitted six air force officers accused of sabotaging planes at the Thornhill base outside Gweru. The defendants had been denied access to counsel and tortured. The judge accepted their evidence that their confessions had been coerced. Even Prime Minister Mugabe admitted that the officers had been tortured, but added that this did not mean that the statements they had made were incorrect. The six were promptly detained under emergency powers. Three were released soon afterwards and expelled from the country. The others remained in detention until the Review Tribunal recommended their release (which suggests that there was no serious evidence against them).

Seven officials of ZAPU were arrested in 1982 after the discovery of arms caches on property owned by the party and were brought to trial in 1983 on charges of treason and illegal possession of arms. Six were acquitted on all counts; the seventh was convicted on the charge of possession of arms. The six were promptly re-detained and at least two of them, Dumiso Dabengwa and Lookout Masuku, were imprisoned for longer than the one, Misheck Velaphi, who was convicted and sentenced to a prison term.**

In 1986 two senior customs officials, Neil Harper and John Austin, were arrested and charged under the Official Secrets Act with spying for South Africa. The Supreme Court released them, finding no reasonable suspicion "such as would make it lawful to deprive them of their liberty." A month later they were re-detained under the Emergency Powers (Maintenance of Law and Order) Regulations and, despite numerous legal challenges, were held without

---

* The full text of the correspondence between Africa Watch and Minister Mahachi is in Appendix A.

** See above.

36

charge until early 1988. Review Tribunal decisions in their favor were overruled by the President.

In a judgment on the Austin and Harper case, Chief Justice Enoch Dumbutshena (who was also judge in the Thornhill trial) stated the judiciary's fears about the arbitrary use of administrative detention:

> Preventive detentions . . . are a matter of constant worry. Sometimes they create unnecessary conflict between the Judiciary, which is the custodian of the rights of citizens who seek protection in the courts, and the Executive, the guardian of the security of the State. When the Executive ignores the orders and judgments of the courts there is an inevitable breakdown of law and order, resulting in uncivilized chaos because the courts cannot enforce their orders. Their jurisdiction and duty end after delivery of judgment.*

Berkeley commented on the Thornhill and Dabengwa cases:

> The most disturbing aspect of these re-detentions is that they are provided for by the Lancaster House Constitution. It is as if the Constitution itself has an escape hatch — it guarantees the right to due process *unless* the Minister of Home Affairs is unhappy with the result.**

For its part the government describes those whom it re-detains as having been acquitted "on technicalities." By that it presumably means that they did in fact commit the crime of which they were accused. In the Dabengwa case the court clearly found that the accused had not done what they were alleged to have done (a conclusion described by the then Minister of Home Affairs as "stranger than fiction"). In the Thornhill trial, the prosecution case rested on the confessions of the accused. Once it was established that these had been extracted under torture they became worthless. Far from being a "technicality," this should have served as an object lesson to the government and CIO that torture is not only inhuman — it is also ineffective. The lesson has not been learned.

---

*   *Minister of Home Affairs & Another v Austin and Another*, S-79-86.

**   Lawyers' Committee, *op cit*, p158.

More recently the pattern has been to avoid cases ever coming to court. Of the cases described above, John Lewis-Walker, Patricia Brown and their co-accused, as well as Leslie Lesia, were all charged under the Official Secrets Act, but charges were withdrawn before they came to trial. Presumably this was because the state had insufficient evidence. In at least three instances — Leslie Lesia, Ivor Harding and Clive Harding — it was probably also because of the fear that evidence of torture would emerge in any public hearing.*

The effect of this in the Lesia case has already been remarked upon: he was held for two years without any sort of review, either judicial or administrative. In the cases of Lewis-Walker and Brown the authorities were initially able to circumvent an unfavorable Review Tribunal decision by charging the prisoners with a criminal offence, and then to issue them with new detention orders when the government was unable to proceed with the charges. This is an abuse of the judicial process, with criminal charges being used as a species of detention order rather than as an impartial means to determine an individual's innocence or guilt.

Equally the swift pardoning of those convicted by the courts can also be an interference with judicial independence, in intent even if not formally. The most striking example of this is the case of the CIO official Robert Masikini, whose case is cited above. He was released under a presidential amnesty only a week after being convicted of murdering a prisoner in his custody. In principle there is little difference between the government re-detaining an innocent person released by the courts and releasing a guilty one.

This interference in the judicial process is regrettable since the formal record of the Zimbabwean Government in respecting judicial independence is creditable. Judges in Zimbabwe are not threatened or intimidated and judicial appointments do not generally appear to have been made on political grounds. The Chief Justice is Enoch Dumbutshena, who has never been a member of the ruling party and who was appointed after acquitting the six Thornhill air force officers. Political (and other) trials are conducted fairly and openly. Perhaps

---

*   For details of the torture inflicted on Ivor and Clive Harding see below, Chapter 5.

the biggest obstacle to the fair administration of justice is not within the government's immediate control. For most Zimbabweans the law is remote and expensive. Most people who are arrested could not contemplate hiring a legal representative – including many who continue to serve sentences for "dissident"-related crimes – and government-funded representation is only provided in the most serious cases. Some private organizations have tried to address this problem: the law faculty of the University of Zimbabwe runs a free legal aid clinic, while the non-governmental Legal Resources Foundation has published a manual for paralegal workers and popular guides to legal issues, as well as running Legal Projects Centers in Harare and Bulawayo.

A worrying recent development has been the use of threats and criminal charges against lawyers acting in important political cases. For instance, in early 1989 Bryant Elliot, the attorney for the Catholic Justice and Peace Commission, was briefly detained by police in Gwanda. He was questioned about a document he had in his possession while representing the commission at an inquest into the death of a man who died in the course of the disturbances in Matabeleland South.

In late 1988 Hugh Bisset, a partner in the Bulawayo law firm Webb, Low and Barry, was charged and convicted of perjury. He had been representing Rory Maguire, who was sentenced to seven years imprisonment for failing to report the presence of South African agents. During Maguire's trial in June 1988, Bisset had taken the witness stand to testify that he had not been present when his client made a warned and cautioned statement to the police. A video recording showed that Bisset had in fact been present when the preamble to the statement had been recorded. Bisset said that he had been confused about when precisely he had been present when giving evidence and the magistrate in the Maguire trial commented that he did not think Bisset was being deliberately untruthful. Bisset was arrested – unlawfully as a magistrate later ruled – and charged with perjury. He was convicted of perjury, a verdict which was finally overturned on appeal to the Supreme Court. It was apparent that Bisset was prosecuted because certain officials were hostile to his role in providing legal representation in a politically sensitive case.

David Coltart, also a partner in Webb, Low and Barry and director of the Bulawayo Legal Projects Center, was charged earlier this year with tampering with witnesses. The charges arose out of a case against his client Stanley Bhebhe, who is the District Administrator of Nkayi in Matabeleland North. Bhebhe had incurred the wrath of the local police on two counts. First, he had lent his assistance to a cooperative farming venture to resettle former "dissidents," supported by a national charity, the Zimbabwe Project. Second, he had complained about police involvement in stock theft. At the end of 1988 police detained Bhebhe and members of his staff. One, named Nkabinde, was ill-treated and forced to make a statement incriminating Bhebhe in theft of a borehole pump and some asbestos sheeting from the cooperative. The Zimbabwe Project had not made any complaint of theft (since they had not been stolen). On 3 January 1989 Bhebhe appeared in court and was refused bail. His lawyer, David Coltart, applied to the High Court for bail on his client's behalf. The police opposed bail on the grounds that Bhebhe would intimidate his employees who were to testify against him and the High Court also refused. Finally the Supreme Court agreed to bail.

During the remand hearings Nkabinde visited Coltart's office and said that he had been intimidated by the police into giving evidence against Bhebhe. Coltart explained that he could not talk to him, since he was acting for Bhebhe and sent him to another lawyer.

On February 3 at a remand hearing the charges against Bhebhe were dropped. Coltart advised him that he could sue the police for damages for wrongful arrest. However, a number of new charges were then brought against Bhebhe. Again some members of Bhebhe's staff, including Nkabinde, visited Coltart's office to give evidence of police intimidation and for a second time he told them that he was unable to meet them. On February 10, Nkabinde was detained by the police. Then on February 19 the police issued a warrant for Coltart's arrest on a charge of tampering with witnesses – meaning Nkabinde and others of Bhebhe's staff. In fact the warrant was incorrectly drawn up and Coltart was not taken into custody but the charges remained. The docket was referred to the Attorney General's office in Harare, which finally decided in May 1989 not to proceed with the charges against either Coltart or Bhebhe.

In this case, unlike Bisset's, there is no suggestion of vindictiveness on the part of the state's law officers, who acted properly throughout and made the correct decision not to proceed with an unsustainable case. The fault lies entirely at the level of the police. During the period when Enos Nkala was Minister of Home Affairs, from mid-1985 to the end of 1987, many of the police posts in rural Matabeleland were assigned to officers who shared Nkala's virulently anti-ZAPU sentiments. Most were not Ndebele officers from the local area. This coincided with an increased role for the police in counterinsurgency after the withdrawal of the Fifth Brigade in 1984. The alleged role of the police in orchestrating "disappearances" of ZAPU officials and local councilors has already been mentioned. The unity agreement and the lifting of repression in Matabeleland has not found favor with these officers, who resent the activities of officials like Stanley Bhebhe, who play an active role in reconciliation, and of human rights lawyers such as David Coltart. A thorough review of the assignment of police personnel in Matabeleland would strengthen the process of reconciliation in the region.

Zimbabwean lawyers are also concerned about the lack of action against government ministers who lied to a judicial commission of inquiry into corruption. Five ministers were forced to resign in early 1989 when the Sandura Commission of Inquiry into illegal car sales found that they had perjured themselves. (For further details, see Chapter 5.) In July, one minister, Frederick Shava, was sentenced to nine months imprisonment for perjury, only to be pardoned by the president. The Attorney General then withdrew the charges against the other former ministers. The decision to pardon Shava was reportedly taken at a meeting of the Politburo of ZANU-PF, a body which contains other former ministers who faced perjury charges. At least one of them, Dzingai Mutumbuka, the former Minister of Higher Education, was apparently present at the meeting. Mugabe subsequently told a press conference:

> Who among us has not lied? Yesterday you were with your
> girlfriend and you told your wife you were with the president.
> Should you get nine months for that?

41

One senior lawyer commented that the dropping of perjury charges "gives *carte blanche* to public officials to lie under oath to judicial bodies."*

*   *The Guardian*, July 21, 1989.

5. TORTURE

There is abundant evidence of the use of torture by the police and CIO from independence until 1986, not least from court records, inquest proceedings and *post mortem* reports. This was outlined in Chapter 1 and has been extensively documented by Amnesty International.* Although the government publicly repudiated Amnesty International's allegations, it did make a serious attempt to improve police behavior. Clear instructions forbidding the use of torture were disseminated throughout the police force and seem to be generally respected. The government is reluctant to claim credit for these improvements, since to do so would be to admit past failings, but these positive steps are nevertheless most welcome.** However, where the government has signally failed to deal with the use of torture is in the CIO. In this chapter we report new evidence of CIO torture.

The case of Leslie Johannes Lesia has already been referred to. He is alleged to have been tortured by the CIO in the old customs section of Central Police Station in Harare by having a wet post office sack placed over his head and being beaten on the feet. He later had both legs smashed by being beaten with pick-axe handles while in CIO custody at Goromonzi detention center outside Harare. Another prisoner who alleges that he was tortured is Philip Conjwayo, who was charged and later convicted of murder in the course of a bombing carried out in Bulawayo on behalf of South African intelligence. (The

---

*   *Memorandum to the Government of the Republic of Zimbabwe*, AI Index: AFR 46/10/86, May 1986. (The memorandum was submitted to Prime Minister Mugabe in January 1986.)

**   Another welcome step is the current move to amend the Criminal Procedure and Evidence Act to abolish the use of whipping as a punishment. This follows a Supreme Court judgment in June 1989 which ruled that the punishment was unconstitutional. One of the judges said: "This conclusion, I am confident, will prove acceptable to all who care for the reputation of the legal system in this country and are anxious for it to be thought humane and civilized. For we must never be content to keep upon our Criminal Code provisions for punishment having their origins in the Dark Ages."

detention of Philip Conjwayo's nephew, Joseph Mujakati, was described in the previous chapter.) Conjwayo, a former Rhodesian Special Branch officer, maintained throughout his remand hearings and trial that he had been tortured by being beaten and half-drowned.

The testimony of one of Conjwayo's co-accused, Kevin Woods, is particularly revealing because he was himself a former CIO officer. Until his retirement in September 1986 he had occupied a senior position in CIO "anti-dissident" operations in Matabeleland. At the time of his arrest in January 1988 his wife and daughters were also detained as a way of bringing pressure on him to confess. At his trial Woods testified that when he saw his wife and daughters being led away weeping with fear, Assistant Commissioner Ndove said to him: "I am so glad you are an ex-member. I cannot remember his exact words but they are to the effect I am so glad you are an ex-member because you know what happens to people who do not cooperate."*

Woods said that during his time with the CIO in Matabeleland he knew of prisoners being tortured at Stops Camp in Bulawayo, at a CIO "fort" in Esigodini and at a Bulawayo house which was used as an interrogation center. (He did not give any indication that he had ever tried to restrain his colleagues from torture.) He continued:

> I was terrified. I knew for sure there would be no hesitation in any of these methods being applied to myself or my wife or children.
>
> I have seen people being assaulted with anything from sticks to pieces of hosepipe.
>
> The subject is always handcuffed and leg ironed while these assaults are taking place, his hands usually behind his back.
>
> These beatings are not restricted to any part of the body, and the subject is thrashed on any exposed area. It is not uncommon during these procedures for the interrogators to kick or boot the subject.

---

* This, and the testimony that follows, is drawn from Woods's sworn evidence at his trial in the Bulawayo High Court in 1988.

I have seen suspects having their heads immersed in buckets of water.

A popular method is the use of water, using a government issue rucksack.

A canvas bag is tied around the suspect's neck. At the entrance of the bag is a string which is used as a tie. The bag, before it is tied around his neck, it is half filled with water. After the kit bag has been secured around his neck, the bag is lifted so the water covers his face.*

Generally a piece of cloth is placed underneath the handcuffs and the leg iron to prevent visible injuries being caused from this.

I have seen suspects having the soles of their feet beaten to the extent that the flesh is bruised so much it has even erupted, burst open.

I have seen people with broken limbs as a result of being struck with a pick handle.**

I have seen electrical connectors from a hand dynamo being placed on the private parts of suspects and the subject being shocked by turning the dynamo, through these electrical connections.

It could be a very short interrogation or it could be something that takes days, but it is never left unfinished.

The subject has to capitulate or he will die.

There was mention from Ndove that my wife and children would be interrogated in front of me, and from my knowledge I have seen women and children being beaten and interrogated to the extremes I have mentioned.

Of course Woods's testimony should be treated with caution, but the torture methods described do correspond with those documented by Amnesty

---

*   Compare P J Mpofu's testimony cited in Chapter 2, as well as a number of cases documented in Amnesty International's *Memorandum* and Berkeley's report for the Lawyers Committee for Human Rights.

**   Compare the reported torture of Leslie Lesia.

International and the Lawyers Committee for Human Rights, as well as by Africa Watch. Woods's wife and daughters were not ill-treated and were released soon afterwards, but this does not alter the fact that such hostage-taking cannot be justified in any circumstances. The wife of another co-accused, Michael Smith, was also detained briefly at the same time, apparently with the same purpose.

Further sworn testimony of torture came in the trial of Odile Harington before the High Court in November 1987. Harington had been recruited by South African intelligence to infiltrate the African National Congress (ANC) in Harare and to send back plans of ANC buildings. The purpose presumably was to facilitate South African military raids on the ANC. Harington was arrested when police intercepted a letter from her containing intelligence on the ANC.

Harington testified that she was tortured during two distinct periods: first, immediately after her arrest for a period of some 12 days. After her first appearance in court on remand she was not tortured; at this time she was in the custody of the police, rather than CIO. On May 6 charges against her were dropped and she was handed over to the CIO again, who illegally detained her for six weeks at Goromonzi, where she testified that she was regularly tortured. Charges were then revived.

During the first period of torture Harington was held in Mabelreign police station in Harare and taken nightly to a place called Daventry House where she was tortured. On the first occasion she describes being beaten over the back and head with a doubled hosepipe. She says she was "forced to stand in a horizontal position with my hands on the ground and my fist stand inwards [sic] and my legs stretched out behind me."* She was "forced to keep in this unnatural position in a very stiff way and if I relaxed in any way I was kicked or beaten." She adds: "Some time in the evening I was beaten on the soles of my feet with rubber coated wiring the thicker black type and a piece of hose-pipe."

---

*   This, and the testimony that follows, is drawn from Harington's sworn evidence at her trial before the Harare High Court in November 1987.

Later the ANC official under whose command Harington had served also took part in the torture:

> My feet were bound together with a belt. My hands were tied behind my back and my feet were forced through the lower ring of the back of the chair and I was severely beaten severely [sic] with the hosepipe by Rafel [the ANC official] and other members of the CIO...I was beaten on the soles of my feet — it was excruciating and because of my screaming they stuffed a dishcloth into my mouth.

On another occasion she was taken into the veld with an ANC official:

> I was blindfolded with a piece of wet hessian. My hands were tied behind my back with a tie and I was made to lie on the back seat of the vehicle. In the bundu I was told to take up a kneeling position. I was led about 50 metres from the vehicles and then my head was ducked under water contained in a plastic container. This ducking took place intermittently for the whole night. I would approach fainting at times and I was struggling violently to get my head out of the water. The container was brought by the ANC official...

> Jeff [a CIO official] is a big man and was sitting on my back so that I could not get my head out...

> I told Jeff that I wanted a doctor and he said to me I would see one the next day and they never came back and I never saw a doctor.

Odile Harington's testimony continues:

> ...towards five o'clock in the morning after a night's interrogation, Jeff told me to remove my tee shirt and then I had to squat and put my arms behind my head for the benefit of the five male interrogators who were present...He told me to lower my trousers until knee level and Mr Moyo...the other CIO officer, tried to stop him but he was brushed aside. He then instructed me to pull open my private parts so that he could firstly look and this was accompanied by insults and he then told me to pull them open again so that he could spit on them.

Harington also testified that she was not fed properly at Mabelreign police station and lost 10 kilograms in weight during her 12 days there.

From February 13 to May 6 she was on remand and properly treated. After the charges were withdrawn she was taken to Goromonzi where she was again in the charge of "Jeff" and the CIO. Harington describes being beaten on May 7 "the most brutally of all":

> The form of beating was that my feet were tied together with a belt as before and my hands were tied behind my back and they used a piece of solid rubber, it was like a baton, not a baton but that sort of format and I was brutally beaten on my feet. On the soles of my feet. It was excruciating. When they were beating me I was lying on the floor. The assault continued for about five minutes I suppose but I mean it would it would stop and start not only once...During one of those beatings I soiled my pants...I was told to go and wash myself and to hurry so that they could continue, I tried to wash myself but I was barely able to walk.

While she was in Goromonzi Harington made two attempts to commit suicide:

> I was pretty desperate at this stage because I knew there was absolutely no way I could ever satisfy these people. They were getting more and more brutal. I got hold of a little marmalade jar which I broke in my cell and I cut myself on the thigh. I would most happily have bled to death that night...

> I was kept in solitary confinement for the rest of my period at Goromonzi. CIO justified that by saying that I wanted to kill myself but I doubt very much if I would not have been in solitary confinement if that incident had not taken place because all of us were kept separately there...

> Towards the end of my incarceration there I developed a nervous disorder where I was continuously vomiting...I took a deliberate overdose of panadol. I was trying to indicate to these people how desperate I was but the only reaction I got was that I was wanting to die with the information.

Towards the end of her period at Goromonzi she was no longer beaten with hosepipes or batons:

> ...Jeff came up with a suitable alternative...which was to make me sit on a chair and my feet were then put through the lower rung of another chair so that my legs were stretched out horizontally and as I have said before he is an enormous man

and he would then sit on my knees which was as excruciating as being beaten on the soles of my feet but no marks were left by that and on another occasion I was hit really hard on the face probably about fifteen times. The last time was with both hands at one time and I nearly blacked out at that stage...

On the May 8 I was burned with cigarettes about seven or eight times on my legs and feet...

I had one very bloodshot eye from one blow I had received from one CIO member and I suffered from diarrhoea for the entire period at Goromonzi. I've still got that at Central [Police Station]. I was not able to walk properly, I was in a sort of drunken state but I think it was due to shock.

This testimony in court is reinforced by similar accounts given in letters written by Harington during her period in police custody, as well as by her complaints to the magistrate at an early remand hearing. Interestingly, Harington's testimony was not contested in court. The trial judge, the Judge President Wilson Sandura, made this comment in his judgment:

...from her evidence it is possible or *likely* [emphasis added] that she may have been subjected to some form of ill treatment by members of the CIO but on the basis of information I have before me I am unable to say as a fact that this took place.

At a minimum Sandura might have been expected to order an investigation into these allegations, which he clearly regarded as credible. What he in fact did was to state that his personal preference would be for Harington to be taken from the court and shot — but that since he could not do this he was sentencing her to the maximum penalty for espionage of 25 years imprisonment. On appeal Chief Justice Dumbtushena was highly critical of Sandura's unjudicial remarks and reduced her sentence to 12 years. He cited her uncontested allegations of torture in mitigation.

It is remarkable that the government appears to have taken no steps to investigate Odile Harington's horrifying allegations, with the aim of bringing those responsible to justice. Not only has "Jeff" not been prosecuted, but he was observed during the trial of Woods, Conjwayo and Smith, sitting in the public gallery. No government that wishes its abhorrence of torture to be taken seriously can continue to employ torturers in positions of responsibility. Unfortunately, as indicated in Chapters 2 and 3, Zimbabwe's record of bringing human rights violators to justice has been poor.

Africa Watch also considers it important that Odile Harington should obtain redress if she was tortured as she alleged. The government has an obligation to investigate her claim. It has not done so, even though her testimony has been a matter of public record for 18 months. Her crime of passing intelligence on ANC houses to Pretoria could have led to great loss of life and cannot possibly be condoned. Yet those who tortured her should be punished and she should be compensated. A particularly appropriate form of compensation would be to commute her sentence on the grounds that since agents of the state inflicted summary and lawless punishment of an extreme kind on her, the state should not also punish her in the manner and to the degree provided by law. She has been punished more than enough for her crime and the illegitimate acts of agents of the state have stripped the state of the legitimacy it would otherwise enjoy in punishing her according to law.

Africa Watch has also obtained testimony of the torture alleged to have been suffered by Ivor Harding and his son Clive Harding, arrested with John Lewis-Walker and Patricia Brown in September 1987 and accused of spying for South Africa. Charges against them were dropped in August 1988 and they remain in detention without trial. Africa Watch has been able to form no opinion as to whether they had in fact engaged in espionage – but while we could not condone such activity it is entirely irrelevant to their right not to be subjected to torture.

Ivor and Clive Harding were arrested in Beitbridge, on the South African border, on 13 September. The next day they were blindfolded, handcuffed and leg-ironed and driven to Bulawayo. At one stage they asked if they could stop to urinate but were told that they should "piss in your pants." Ivor Harding was taken to Entumbane police station and Clive to Stops Camp. Both men were repeatedly refused access to a lawyer.

Two days after their arrest the Hardings were taken separately to a private house in Lotus Drive, Bulawayo, where they were each interrogated by the CIO. Clive Harding states:

I was taken in to the kitchen and tied on to the chair. My legs were tied to the feet of the chair and my arms were tied to the armrests. I heard my father speaking where I was sitting. The CIO members questioned me. I told them that I was working for CIO officials in Harare and was doing foreign affairs outside Zimbabwe. The CIO members did not believe me. One member took out the Swiss pocket knife and pliers and stated that if I did not say what he wanted to hear, he would show me "some of our tactics." The CIO members started off by extracting the entire nail on the big toe on my right foot, and then proceeded to extract my entire finger nail on my left hand [sic]. I was thereafter taken to the sitting room where I saw my father, and my father said that I must admit to anything that I was asked.

According to Ivor Harding, he had arrived before Clive, had been kicked in the stomach and made to undress. He had been handcuffed while the bath was filled with water. He was put in the bath. One CIO officer pressed down on his chest whilst another lifted up Ivor Harding's legs, submerging his head. He was ducked repeatedly and was afraid that he was going to drown. He was then made to dress and Clive arrived. Ivor could hear Clive's screams in the next room and said that he would admit to anything if they would stop torturing his son.

On his return to Entumbane police station Ivor Harding collapsed from internal bleeding and was taken to a private clinic. Despite the recommendation of the doctor there, he was not admitted to hospital. On September 18 the Hardings were taken to Harare, where Ivor was examined at Parirenyatwa hospital. They were then taken to Goromonzi detention center and Ivor was not taken for further examination at Parirenyatwa as the doctor had recommended. However, he did receive some medication, but Ivor suspects that one of the drugs that he was given was intended to make him suggestible and that he made a false statement while under its influence.

The Hardings allege that at Goromonzi they were kept for almost 24 hours a day in total darkness. There were six small, windowless cells, with no beds. If they were thirsty they were obliged to drink from the lavatory in the cell. This corresponds to other accounts of conditions in Goromonzi. Ivor Harding

51

maintains that a bone in his left hand was broken after he was beaten with handcuffs.

Clive Harding states:

The cell that I was placed in was covered in blood from an African male, by the name of Jackson who was murdered on September 5, 1987 by CIO members. I was still tortured at Goromonzi cells even after admitting to what the CIO wanted to hear. I was taken to Goromonzi Clinic for treatment for my nose and at one stage I thought that the CIO had damaged my appendix. The CIO members frequently had their AK-47 rifles pointed and cocked at my chest and said that I could die at any minute. They also said that no one would know if I was killed. Mr Reed [CIO official] took me to a house the following day and sat me in a dining room chair and began to beat me about the face with a doubled up army belt. The guards at Goromonzi cells were very hostile and at one stage tried to put a bayonet into me and I avoided it by jumping back just in time. The guard then cocked his AK rifle and I asked him to shoot me in order for the matter to be over with as I was fed up, very sick and was full of pain.

On another occasion:

I told Mr Reed all that I knew but he continued to be hostile and thereafter I told him to go to hell. He then ordered one of his fellow workmates to hit me on the shins with a Coke bottle and I still have the scar.

The Hardings had no access to a lawyer for three weeks to a month after their arrest.

Africa Watch cannot corroborate Ivor and Clive Harding's allegations of torture, but several observations can be made. First, the long delay in giving the Hardings access to a lawyer — when the Emergency Powers (Maintenance of Law and Order) Regulations stipulate that a detainee can see a lawyer "without delay" — suggests that the CIO had some reason for wishing that they did not receive outside visits. Second, their accounts of torture correspond in various respects to testimonies gathered by Amnesty International and the Lawyers Committee for Human Rights. Third, both Ivor and Clive Harding received medical examinations at various stages during their detention — in

Bulawayo, at Parirenyatwa hospital and at the Goromonzi clinic. Methods such as water torture have been used specifically because they do not leave signs which could be used as later evidence of torture. However other injuries, such as Ivor's broken bone in the hand and Clive's extracted finger and toenails, should have been recorded in medical examinations and would therefore be available to any subsequent investigation. If records of the medical examinations were not available, then investigators might draw conclusions from that.

To Africa Watch's knowledge the Zimbabwean Government has not at any stage established an independent inquiry into allegations of torture, despite extensive evidence that torture has taken place and the fact that an investigatory mechanism exists under the country's Commissions of Inquiry Act. When Amnesty International called on the government to set up such an inquiry in 1985, the then Minister of Home Affairs responded by saying that it was the responsibility of those who alleged that they had been tortured to make a complaint to the authorities. In fact there are a variety of reasons why torture victims may not make a complaint. One is the fear of reprisals from those responsible for the torture. Another is the emotional or psychological condition of the victim. A third is that the victim may have died as a result of torture. The Declaration against Torture adopted by the UN General Assembly in 1975 recognizes that governments have an obligation to investigate serious reports of torture even if the victim has not complained:

> Wherever there is reasonable ground to believe that an act of torture...has been committed, the competent authorities of the State concerned shall promptly proceed to an impartial investigation even if there has been no formal complaint. [Article 9]

In Zimbabwe there is considerable sworn testimony in affidavits and court records, as well as *post mortem* reports and inquest proceedings, which provide *prima facie* evidence of the need for such an inquiry. There is no indication that those who have publicly complained of torture, such as Odile Harington or Kembo Mohadi, a ZAPU MP detained in 1985, have had their allegations investigated.

The evidence we have cited suggests that torture has continued since the political rapprochement between ZANU-PF and ZAPU. However, the freer atmosphere since the unity agreement makes it easier for these matters to be aired publicly. A commission of inquiry, followed by prosecutions of torturers, would be an important sign that torture is not officially tolerated, as well as deterring its use in future.

6. FREEDOM OF EXPRESSION:
POLITICAL OPPOSITION, THE PRESS
AND HUMAN RIGHTS MONITORING

Since before independence Mugabe's ZANU-PF has made clear its intention that Zimbabwe should be a one-party state. The independence constitution agreed with Britain at Lancaster House in 1979 guarantees the preservation of a multi-party political system until 1990 — 10 years after independence — unless all members of parliament agree to it. For his part, President Mugabe has said that a one-party system will not be introduced without popular support.

The move towards a one-party system has considerable symbolic importance for defenders of Rhodesia, who like to maintain that the maintenance of institutionalized racism was in fact a defence of Western democratic values against Marxist tyranny — as if those values could be reconciled with the refusal to count persons equally by reason of race. However, this view does not have wide currency among Zimbabwe's remaining white population of around 100,000. Mugabe's government has assiduously wooed the whites because of their significant economic role. A number of white farmers have joined ZANU-PF and, at the national level, Mugabe has succeeded in attracting the support of long-standing members of Ian Smith's Rhodesian Front, notably former Justice Minister Chris Andersen and Charles Duke, both of whom hold ministerial posts. In 1987, at the earliest opportunity constitutionally available to it, the government introduced an important democratic reform by abolishing the 20 per cent of parliamentary seats reserved exclusively for whites. No general election has been held since then, although any political party, including a one with a predominantly white membership, is at present entitled to contest any parliamentary seat.

Since independence the principal minority party has been Joshua Nkomo's ZAPU. The ruling ZANU was a breakaway from ZAPU in 1963 and relations between the two parties were soured by the conflicts and rivalries that had created the original split. To these had been added an ethnic factor, with ZANU-PF drawing most of its support from the Shona-speaking east and north, while ZAPU was strong among Sindebele-speakers in the south-west. As armed conflict broke out in Matabeleland, the government and its supporters generally perceived ZAPU as the political wing of the armed rebels. The party was severely repressed, making normal multiparty politics impossible. The unity agreement between the two parties in December 1987, followed by the May 1988 amnesty, restored a measure of normal political debate. But it was widely assumed at the time that unity of the parties was merely a step on the path to the one-party state.

Since the unity agreement, however, there has been a transformation of the country's political life. The breakdown of traditional party rivalries has allowed the emergence of a vigorously critical backbench in the House of Assembly which has been prepared to confront the government on issues ranging from human rights abuse to corruption. (However, the backbench is as yet small — a majority of members of parliament are government ministers!) Even more important has been the growth of popular dissatisfaction with the ostentation and corruption of some government and party leaders — the so-called *chefs*. Hence there has developed a popular opposition to the one-party state. It can be safely assumed that for the most part the objections are not philosophical but stem from the enormous gulf between the living standards of the *chefs* and those of the mass of people. Mugabe's assurance that the one-party state will not be imposed thus assumes practical importance, although it is not clear what it actually means. Will there be a referendum on the constitutional change? If so what majority would be required? Will the government wait for the withering away of other parties? Or will it in some unspecified way gauge when the popular mood is favorable.

The crucial distinction between ZANU-ZAPU unity and the introduction of a one-party state were well stated in a recent editorial in the Catholic magazine *Moto*:

Of late it has increasingly seemed as if unity is synonymous
with the one-party state in Zimbabwe, and that those who

56

might want to form another political party are against national unity. That is unfortunate, particularly when people get emotionally charged about these issues.

We admit the distinction is very thin. Still, a distinction there is. Our leaders have assured us again and again that a one-party state will not be imposed on the people without their consent. In other words, people would have to be consulted — asked to make a definite decision for or against the one-party state....

It will be a sad day when in our beloved motherland opinions divergent from the "party line" can only be whispered fearfully. Politicians have a heavy responsibility — not only as national leaders, but also as Members of Parliament — to respect the political will of the people. The future of democracy in Zimbabwe is being decided now.*

Moto's point is especially apt since the formation in April 1989 of the Zimbabwe Unity Movement (ZUM). ZUM's leader is a former secretary-general of ZANU-PF, Edgar Tekere. As described in Chapter 3, Tekere was removed from party and government posts in 1981 after his acquittal on a technicality of murdering a white farmer the previous year. However, Tekere remained influential among the left wing of the ruling party and particularly in his home area of Manicaland on the eastern border, where he was provincial party chairman. He criticized corruption and the size of government, as well as increasingly distancing himself from the move towards a one-party state. In early 1988 he was removed from the leadership of ZANU-PF in Manicaland. Then, in October 1988, he made a speech fiercely attacking government corruption. However, he went a step further than any previous critics by placing some of the blame on Mugabe for failing to remove corrupt members of government. The Central Committee of ZANU-PF promptly voted to expel him.

The episode was revealing because the defenders of single-party systems argue that criticism can be contained and encompassed within the

---

* *Moto*, No 77, June 1989.

framework of the ruling party. Yet here was a demonstration that as soon as anyone overstepped an invisible line he would be removed. This was not intrinsically surprising: as early as 1985 a group of ZANU-PF trade unionists who criticized corruption among their union leadership were detained for some weeks. However, Tekere's expulsion did as much as any single episode to illustrate to ordinary Zimbabweans the dangers of the one-party state.

Tekere did not instantly follow the advice of his followers, who included a vocal group of students at the University of Zimbabwe, and set up a new party. By the time he finally did, Mugabe had made his own moves against corruption and taken some of the wind out of Tekere's sails. Publicly the ruling party declared itself unconcerned by the formation of ZUM, although many column inches in the government press were devoted to the new party's alleged links to die-hard Rhodesians and South Africa.

However, despite their professed indifference, the authorities instantly began a sustained campaign of harassment against ZUM. The first two months of its existence were particularly sensitive because they coincided with a parliamentary by-election in Harare's Dzivarasekwa constituency, which ZUM contested. The ZANU-PF candidate was declared to have won, with ZUM polling 28 per cent of the votes cast. Tekere alleged that two government ministers had illegally entered polling stations to intimidate voters, and that party loyalists had been bussed in from outside the constituency to vote. Africa Watch cannot confirm these allegations. However, there must be serious doubts about the fairness of the election campaign. The first two ZUM election meetings at Highfield and Mabvuku — the first public meetings in the party's history — were banned by the police. A subsequent rally in Chitungwiza was called off because ZUM supporters were locked out of the stadium where it was to be held. The chairman of Chitungwiza Town Council, Forbes Magadu, said that the gates were locked because ZUM had not paid a deposit. ZUM officials said that the Town Council had refused to accept the deposit from them. The same Forbes Magadu is also ZANU-PF political commissar for Harare and played a prominent part in the Dzivarasekwa campaign. At the same time security officials prevented members of the public from attending a meeting to launch ZUM in Bulawayo, and a ZUM official was subsequently charged with convening a public meeting without authority. A ZUM official also alleged that the managing director of the official Zimbabwe Newspapers had stopped an advertisement for a later ZUM rally in Bulawayo from appearing in the *Chronicle* newspaper.

On June 6, 1989 prominent ZUM member Freddie Madenge was arrested in Harare. Davison Gomo, a senior party spokesperson, Lazarus Mutungwazi, James Dzova and 11 others were arrested two days later. They were held without charge at Harare Central Police Station. Unusually, Home Affairs Minister Moven Mahachi responded publicly to Africa Watch appeals on behalf of the 15 detained ZUM members:

> There is freedom to form political parties but there is no freedom to subvert a legitimate Government. We will not hesitate to pick anybody up as long as we have reasonable grounds that they are engaged in subversive activities.*

In fact the 15 were released a few days later without charge, suggesting that the grounds for detaining them were not so reasonable.

On July 18, 1989 Tekere was still trying to address his first public meeting since ZUM's formation. That evening armed police dispersed 5,000 students who were attending a rally addressed by Tekere at the University of Zimbabwe. Police fired teargas into students' dormitories.

On October 6-7, 1989, 11 ZUM members were arrested in Chinhoyi, some 70 miles from Harare. They included the party's provincial secretary for Mashonaland West, Cornelius Watama. At the time of writing they had apparently not been charged and had not seen a lawyer. A ZUM spokesperson also alleged that a store owned by a party supporter had been stoned by members of the Youth League of the ruling party.

When a newly formed party can win nearly a third of the vote in ZANU-PF's Harare stronghold, President Mugabe may take this as evidence that the public is not yet won over to the idea of the one-party state. However, it is worrying that in the first two months of the new party's existence it has suffered repeated harassment and detentions. The government is apparently

---

*   *Manica Post*, June 30, 1989.

59

unaware of any contradiction between this and its verbal assurances that anyone is free to form a political party.

A recent development which has concerned some observers is the transfer of responsibility for the Youth Wing and Women's League of the ruling party away from the relevant Ministries (Youth, Sport and Culture and Community and Women's Affairs) into the Ministry of Political Affairs. The fear is that in the period leading up to the next general election in 1990 these wings of the party will be engaged in violence and intimidation of political opponents. Such fears are not fanciful, since this is precisely what happened around the last general election in 1985. Supporters of ZAPU were forcibly bussed to ZANU-PF rallies, beaten up, had their homes burned down and in a few instances were killed.* Members of the Youth Wing were among those released under the June 1988 presidential amnesty. In September 1988 the Attorney General instructed the prosecution to drop all charges during the trial of 13 youths from the ruling party alleged to have burned down and destroyed property owned by ZAPU members. The inference is that the government treats such behavior lightly. In a plural society it is highly questionable whether such party bodies should fall under the control of any Ministry; at election time it creates the appearance that supposedly impartial state organs are favoring one party against the others.

Those who criticize from outside the framework of party politics scarcely fare better than members of minority parties. In September 1988 students at the University of Zimbabwe and Harare Polytechnic attempted to organize a demonstration against corruption. However, the police prevented the demonstration from leaving the campuses and broke up the protests with teargas and baton charges. The demonstrators declared their loyalty to President Mugabe and were taken aback when he returned from an overseas trip to endorse the harsh police action. Law lecturer Shadreck Gutto, a Kenyan political exile, was summarily expelled from the country because he was alleged to have helped the students draft an anti-corruption manifesto. Four other

---

* For details see International Human Rights Law Group, *Zimbabwe: Report on the 1985 General Elections* and Lawyers' Committee, *op cit*, pp113-134.

lecturers, along with six students, were charged under the Law and Order (Maintenance) Act with inciting public violence. The charges were later dropped, but the 15 members of the university Students' Representative Council had their grants withdrawn by the government in January 1989, apparently because they had circulated documents which were said to be offensive to the office of the President. Two months later the grants were restored after the students wrote a letter of apology to the Minister of Higher Education. In many respects the withdrawal of the grants was a more serious sanction than the criminal charges. To cut off the students' means of livelihood was a harsher penalty than anything the courts were likely to impose. Also the criminal charges were unlikely ever to succeed in court, whereas the withdrawal of the grants was an administrative measure for which the authorities were not required to give a reason. The calculated humiliation of the students by their letter of apology does not enhance either intellectual freedom at the university or political freedom in the country at large.

In June 1989, one of the four lecturers who had been charged, Kempton Makamure, acting Dean of the Faculty of Law, was arrested and detained for a week at Harare's Marimba police station. The Emergency Powers (Maintenance of Law and Order) Regulations require that written reasons for detention must be served within seven days of a person's arrest. Since Makamure was released just within that time limit, the reasons for his detention were never officially stated. Apart from his alleged involvement in the anti-corruption protest, Makamure had offended the government in May 1989 when he gave a radio interview to the official Zimbabwe Broadcasting Corporation criticizing the country's new investment code. The code, which liberalized foreign exchange requirements for overseas companies and facilitated the repatriation of profits, was generally welcomed in Western economic circles but criticized by the Zimbabwean left. The two journalists who interviewed Makamure, Robin Shava and Nyika Bara, were suspended from their posts.*

---

*   See below.

61

On September 29, 1989 students at the university attempted to hold a seminar to mark the first anniversary of their anti-corruption demonstration. Some 200 riot police and the CIO members arrived on campus to disperse 300 students, telling them that their gathering was illegal. On October 2 the Students' Representative Council (SRC) issued a statement protesting the police action as a violation of academic freedom. In the early hours of October 4, police again came onto campus to arrest Arthur Mutambara, SRC president, and Enoch Chikweche, the organization's secretary general. Mutambara was injured trying to escape arrest.

As news of the arrests spread, thousands of students assembled to protest, according to reports in the government-owned press. In the course of this spontaneous demonstration a Mercedes Benz car belonging to Vice-Chancellor Walter Kamba was damaged. At least 70 students were arrested. Later the same day Professor Kamba announced that the university was being closed indefinitely, the first time this had happened since independence in 1980. Kamba, who is known to be a close advisor of Mugabe, refused to condemn either the initial police action against the seminar or the arrest of the student union officials. Students were given only a few hours to leave campus. The term had only just started and students had not yet received their grant payments, so many were stranded in Harare with no money. The closure, carried out in consultation with President Mugabe who is chancellor of the university, drew condemnation from the University Teachers' Association and the University Senate.

Most of the students arrested on October 4 had been released by the end of the week, but six remain in detention at the time of writing. Apart from the two SRC officials they are: Christopher Giwa, Peter Myabo, Edmore Tobaiwa and Samuel Simango. They are apparently held under 30-day detention orders issued under the Emergency Powers (Maintenance of Law and Order) Regulations at various police stations in the Harare area.

Labor rights

Trade union rights, particularly for the black majority, were severely curtailed before independence. There has been a significant growth in trade unionism since 1980 and the emergence of a single trade union confederation, the Zimbabwe Congress of Trade Unions, which is often critical of government policy. However, under the 1985 Labor Relations Act the right to strike remains limited by lengthy negotiating procedures which must be exhausted before a strike can be regarded as legal.* The most serious threat to workers' rights lies in the prohibition under several different laws, including the Labor Relations Act, of the right of workers in "essential services" to withdraw their labor.

As in other areas, the Zimbabwean Government inherited repressive laws enacted by the Rhodesian regime which it has since added to. The Emergency Powers Act defined essential services as hospitals, transport, electricity, water, sewerage, food, fuel, coal, fire brigade, coal mining and communications. These can be widened by notice in the Government Gazette. By a notice of 1965, which is still in force, finance, commerce and industry are all defined as essential services. The Law and Order (Maintenance) Act, dating from 1960, prescribes a maximum five-year prison sentence for incitement to strike in an essential service (section 32) and ten years for interfering with an essential service (section 34).

In May 1989 junior doctors went on strike throughout the country in protest at pay and conditions of service. Many were arrested and 77 of them charged under sections 32 and 34 of the Law and Order (Maintenance) Act, although charges were later withdrawn after Mugabe himself had intervened to defuse the situation. However, as an apparent consequence of the doctors' strike, the government introduced new regulations under the Emergency Powers Act, which like the Law and Order (Maintenance) Act, outlaw strikes in "essential services." Since the definition of essential services in force is still that of the 1965 government notice, in effect any worker who goes on strike can be charged under the Emergency Powers (Maintenance of Essential Services) Regulations, 1989, and will face a prison sentence of up to two years.

---

*   In 1987 the government's Secretary for Labor is reported as saying: "All strikes since I took office have been illegal because I have not approved any strikes." Cited by Brian Wood, "Trade Union Organization and the Working Class" in Colin Stoneman (ed), *Zimbabwe's Prospects*, Macmillan, London 1988, p304.

In August 1989 the new regulations were tried out for the first time against striking railway artisans. Then technicians at the Posts and Telecommunications Corporation (PTC) in Harare went on strike over a pay grievance. Telecommunications workers elsewhere in the country began a go-slow. By the first week in September, 116 PTC employees had been arrested and charged with breach of the new regulations. The lawyer for some of the accused argued that the regulations were in breach of the constitutional provision prohibiting forced labor.

As with the use of detention without trial, this appears to be an abuse of the use of emergency powers. The striking telecommunications workers have no connection with either the insurgency in Manicaland or South African espionage — the two stated reasons for maintaining the emergency.

One leading PTC striker, Lovemore Matombo, was detained for a week under the Emergency Powers (Maintenance of Law and Order) Regulations and released just before the authorities were required to provide written reasons for his imprisonment.

After the closure of the university on October 4, the Zimbabwe Congress of Trade Unions issued a statement condemning the action of the Vice-Chancellor and government, under the name of its general secretary Morgan Tsvangirai. On the morning of October 6, the CIO arrested Tsvangirai; later that day he was taken, barefoot and handcuffed, to his office, which the CIO officials proceeded to search. He was taken away and, at the time of writing, had not been seen again. On October 11, the High Court issued an order compelling the CIO to give Tsvangirai's lawyer access to him within 24 hours. Shortly after Tsvangirai's arrest, two other senior union officials were briefly detained for questioning. They were Andrew Ganya, organizing secretary of the Plastics, Chemical and Allied Workers Union, and Trust Ngirande, organizing secretary of the National Leatherworkers' Union.

Freedom of the press

In February 1989 Geoffrey Nyarota, editor of the official *Chronicle* newspaper in Bulawayo, found himself promoted to the newly created post of group public relations officer in Harare. The *Chronicle* had exposed a major corruption scandal in which government ministers were buying cars from Harare's Willowvale assembly plant and reselling them at vast profit above the legally controlled price. As a result President Mugabe set up a judicial commission of inquiry which led to the resignation of several ministers.

Nyarota's deputy at the *Chronicle*, Davison Maruziva, was also promoted to become deputy editor of the *Herald* in Hararc, which has been uncritical of any aspect of government policy or behavior. The *Chronicle* has published no more corruption scoops under its new editor, Stephen Mpofu.

Under Nyarota and Maruziva, the *Chronicle* had provided chapter and verse for the allegations of corruption made by the students and Edgar Tekere. They were immensely popular and hence difficult to sack. Instead they were subjected to what one backbench member of parliament called "elimination by promotion."

Almost inevitably the Willowvale car scandal was dubbed "Willowgate." It came to light quite by accident in October 1988. Bulawayo businessman Obert Mpofu, who is also a member of parliament, received an unexpected cheque for nearly $4,000 from the Willowvale company. It was actually intended for one Alford Mpofu, an employee of Manilal Naran who is a close friend of the then Industry Minister Callistus Ndlovu. (Naran had bought a $60,000 Bulawayo house for his friend, who was the minister responsible for the government-owned Willowvale plant. He was later arrested for foreign exchange offenses.)

Alford Mpofu and another Naran employee, Don Ndlovu, had been allocated Mazda pick-up trucks from Willowvale on Naran's behalf. They had paid in advance but when they went to collect them Mpofu had been allocated a cheaper model. Hence the refund, which was sent to the wrong Mpofu.*

The exposure of "Willowgate" was not apparently intended to embarrass the government, since both the original source and the journalist responsible are thoroughly loyal to Mugabe. Obert Mpofu, a government member of parliament, took his story to Nyarota, a former Mugabe press secretary. The

---

* The *Chronicle*, October 21, 1988, December 10, 1988.

65

Chronicle pursued the affair vigorously over the weeks that followed, publishing long lists of ministers who had been allocated Willowvale vehicles — and details of how these were resold illegally for two or three times the official price. Apart from Industry Minister Ndlovu, those implicated included two of Mugabe's most senior advisers: Minister of Defence Enos Nkala and Senior Minister for Political Affairs Maurice Nyagumbo.

Most Zimbabweans have a healthy skepticism towards the official news media, but retain a voracious appetite for real news. The *Herald*'s dismal record for serious reporting has led to a flourishing of independent news magazines such as *Parade* and *Prize Africa*, which mix sport, fashion and showbiz gossip with serious political journalism. The country's three daily papers, the *Herald*, the *Chronicle* and the *Manica Post*, are all government controlled, as are the *Sunday Mail* (Harare) and the *Sunday News* (Bulawayo) and two Shona and Sindebele-language weeklies. The weekly *Financial Gazette* is independent and critical, but has a small print run and is aimed largely at the white community. The Catholic monthly magazine *Moto* is perhaps the most important forum for critical ideas. There is undoubtedly the market for a non-government daily newspaper with an independent editorial line. However, the existing dailies run at a loss and are heavily subsidized. There is no independent financial backer prepared to incur the government's wrath by launching a new paper. Thus the most important print media remain under effective government control. The radio, which is the most important news medium in a predominantly rural society with a low level of literacy, is tightly controlled. Thus the emergence of Nyarota's *Chronicle* as an investigative newspaper won it an enthusiastic readership in Harare, as well as Bulawayo. As the Willowvale story developed, long queues would form in the capital to await the *Chronicle*'s mid-morning arrival.

In November the *Chronicle* was engaged in a further clash with government. A reporter, Gibbs Dube, accompanied by a driver named Philip Maseko, visited the home of the governor of Matabeleland South, Mark Dube, to interview him about illegal gold-mining in Esigodini. (The two Dubes are not related.) The interview had been arranged by Geoffrey Nyarota. When they had seen the governor, Gibbs Dube and Maseko began the drive back to Bulawayo. Mark Dube's car overtook them and the governor and his security men flagged them down, seized their car keys and ordered them into his vehicle. They were driven back to the governor's house. Gibbs Dube said afterwards:

> The governor accused me of trying to discredit him. He accused me of publishing sensational news which he said was not true. Then he started to assault me. He hit me twice with a clenched fist.
>
> He then tried to throw a beer bottle at me, but was restrained by one of the two men who were in the house.
>
> Then he left for his bedroom where he said he was going to fetch his gun to shoot me so that there would be big news to write about.
>
> He then came for me again, but his friends restrained him. Then he went for Cde Maseko and started assaulting him with his fist. At that point I ran away and made good my escape.*

Maseko was handed over to the custody of the Esigodini police, who held him for some hours — while denying to the *Chronicle* that they had any knowledge of him.

All this was too much even for the management of Zimbabwe Newspapers. The group's chief executive, Elias Rusike, observed that if Mark Dube went unpunished, "Zimbabwe may be entering a new frightening era when the rights of ordinary citizens are trampled underfoot willy-nilly by those in authority."** Likewise deputy commissioner of police Douglas Chingoka criticized police at Esigodini for detaining Maseko on Governor Dube's orders: "The police should protect people and should not get unlawful orders as no one is above the law."***

Mugabe's reaction was quite different. He spent a press conference attacking "over zealous" reporters and repeating Mark Dube's extraordinary allegation that the two *Chronicle* men had gone to the governor's house secretly,

---

*   The *Herald*, November 28, 1988.

**   The *Herald*, November 29, 1988.

***   The *Herald*, November 30, 1988.

disguised as gardeners. "A governor must be dignified," Mugabe said, "but this does not mean that there was no provocation."* In September 1989 a Bulawayo magistrates' court found Governor Dube guilty of assault and fined him $150.

At about the same time Joseph Polizzi, a reporter who had covered "Willowgate" for the *Chronicle*'s sister paper, the *Sunday News*, narrowly escaped when a car drove at him as he left the office one night. He suffered bruising. Previously Polizzi had been arrested after he had dressed as a doctor in an attempt to enter Bulawayo city morgue to investigate a story. Polizzi alleges that he was assaulted and is suing the police. He was detained for eight days without charge.**

A fortnight after the Dube assault, Davison Maruziva telephoned Enos Nkala, the Minister of Defence, to seek his reaction to allegations that he was involved in the Willowvale racket. Nkala's response is worth quoting at length:

> Where did you get that information? That information is supposed to be with the police and the president. I want that information here in my office. Who do you think you are?

> If you do not travel here [to Harare] I will teach each of you a lesson. I will use the army to pick you up and then you can ask your questions; I do not care...

> Do not play that kind of game with me. I am not [Callistus] Ndlovu...I am not the kind to play with. Play with anybody else. I am giving you an ultimatum: if by tomorrow you do not come back to me to say you are coming, then you will come by other means.

> I have got that power. I will lock you up, along with your editor who gave you that information. That question must be answered. I am the acting Minister of Home Affairs and I am instructing the police to search your offices and you can write that.***

---

*   *Ibid.*

**   *New York Times*, January 20, 1989.

***   The *Chronicle*, December 14, 1988.

From the safety of hindsight, this sounds like bluster. Nkala lied to the commission of inquiry into corruption and was forced to resign. At the time however, since the Minister of Home Affairs was out of the country, Nkala was in charge of both army and police. It was he who threatened in 1986 that anyone who sent information to Amnesty International would be locked up. And to prove that he meant it he ordered the detention of the head of Zimbabwe's leading human rights organization. Just two weeks beforehand, a member of the government had beaten up a reporter and apparently got away with it. Maruziva was entitled to feel scared.

Nyarota later related, in sworn testimony to the commission of inquiry.

Some people came to warn us personally that this was no longer safe for us and in fact in due course the chairman of the Zimbabwe Mass Media Trust [the major shareholder in Zimbabwe Newspapers] summoned me to Harare and indicated that reaction was very strong at this point from certain government ministers.

He told me he had called me up for my safety, that he understood that there were instructions that I should be first dismissed from work and subsequently arrested. He called me to Harare so that I would be safe here.

I did confirm that Callistus Ndlovu, who, while the Information Minister had been away had been appointed acting minister, had issued instructions to the Zimbabwe Mass Media Trust that I should be dismissed immediately, which move the trust resisted.*

At the end of December Mugabe finally appointed a commission of inquiry, headed by Justice Wilson Sandura, although there was still a widespread view that it would be a whitewash. As it turned out, the commission held well-attended and highly theatrical hearings in Harare, where ministers such as Nkala and Ndlovu endured a merciless public inquisition. By the time the commission had reported, five ministers and a provincial governor had been

---

* The *Chronicle*, January 27, 1989.

forced to resign. One minister, Maurice Nyagumbo, committed suicide by drinking pesticide.

This should have been Nyarota's hour of glory. However, in January —shortly after the Sandura commission was established —Information Minister Witness Mangwende announced his intention of "examining the structures" of the Mass Media Trust. Restructuring, it soon emerged, simply meant moving Nyarota and Maruziva where they could do no harm. Nyarota was moved to a previously unheard of public relations job and Maruziva soon followed him to Harare. Formally, of course, these were promotions. But even Mugabe himself seemed to have difficulty in getting his story straight. He said that no one would complain about getting a higher salary, but at the same time criticized Nyarota for "overzealousness." But if Mugabe was uncertain whether Nyarota's removal was punishment or reward, the message conveyed to the public was clear: Nyarota was promoted because he went too far.

Nyarota's removal aroused considerable public concern. Backbench member of parliament Byron Hove raised the matter in the House of Assembly. Ministers closed ranks, repeating the universal refrain of the government censor: they did not object to criticism, but it had to be constructive. Thus Sydney Sekeramayi, the Minister of State for National Security: "I want to stand here and make it very clear that some of us do not condone corruption at all and to the extent that the press exposes corruption, we are with it. But to the extent that the press now deliberately target Government as its enemy, then we part ways."*

In the course of his contribution to the parliamentary debate on Nyarota's removal, Byron Hove quoted from a pamphlet by Mikhail Gorbachev: "Criticism is a bitter medicine, but the ills that plague society make it a necessity. Those who think that criticism need only be dosed out at intervals are wrong. People who are inclined to believe stagnation has been fully overcome and it is time to take it easy are just as wrong. A slackening of criticism will inevitably

---

*   *Zimbabwe: Parliamentary Debates*, February 15, 1989.

harm *glasnost* and *perestroika.*"* A few weeks later Hove was advertized to address the Britain-Zimbabwe Society on the theme of "The need for *glasnost* and *perestroika* in Zimbabwe." The meeting never took place, after ZANU-PF Politburo member Didymus Mutasa had intervened to stop it.

Nyarota is the third editor to have been removed from his post for offending the government. His removal, like the previous ones, raises important questions about who controls the press in Zimbabwe. At independence in 1980 the government, with the help of a Nigerian grant, bought out the South African owners of the *Herald*, *Chronicle* and *Manica Post* and their Sunday counterparts and set up a Mass Media Trust as principal shareholder in Zimbabwe Newspapers (1980) Ltd. The trustees are supposed to represent the people of Zimbabwe and the trust objects strenuously when the newspapers are described as government-owned. But in practice it is clear that the Minister of Information plays the decisive role in hiring and firing senior staff.

In July 1985 Elias Rusike, head of Zimbabwe Newspapers, wrote to Willie Musarurwa, removing him from the editorial chair at the *Sunday Mail* because: "The Government, through the Minister of Information, Posts and Telecommunications, has taken the view that the *Sunday Mail*, under your editing, has acted like an opposition newspaper." Musarurwa's principal offence seems to have been to report a financial scandal at the national airline, Air Zimbabwe. The then Minister of Information, Nathan Shamuyarira, had repeatedly criticized Musarurwa, who before his appointment had been a ZAPU member. The country's most experienced editor, Musarurwa no longer has a regular job in journalism.

In 1987 Musarurwa's successor at the *Sunday Mail*, Henry Muradzikwa, ran a story about Zimbabwean students being deported from Cuba allegedly because they were suffering from AIDS. The story coincided with the visit to Harare of a top Cuban official who objected to it. Mugabe publicly pledged: "I shall deal with him personally." Muradzikwa, like Nyarota, was removed to a

---

*   *Ibid.*

non-editorial post. The Mass Media Trust does not seem to have been consulted.

On May 18, 1989 Robin Shava and Nyika Bara of the Zimbabwe Broadcasting Corporation interviewed Kempton Makamure on the new investment code for the Radio 4 program entitled "Gate." According to Byron Hove, who subsequently raised the matter in parliament, the following day the two journalists were hauled up before Information Minister Mangwende and asked why they had "picked on Makamure who is in opposition to Government." In a letter from the Senior Controller of Radio Services the two were suspended from duties with effect from May 23.*

Replying to Hove, Mangwende's deputy Kenneth Manyonda made the customary disclaimer of government involvement in the suspensions, but then told Parliament: "It is not that the Code should not be criticized, but that it should be criticized knowledgeably."

He went on: "Any journalist who is worth his salt should know that there are two sides to any story, and considering that the Investment Code is what everybody was waiting for it was only proper for the press to play its role positively by giving those involved equal and ideally the first opportunity to inform and educate the public."** This is a curious comment, given that the press had spent the previous few weeks giving the code enthusiastic mentions at every opportunity. The interview with Makamure was probably the first contrary view to be heard in the official media. Makamure's prior involvement with student criticism was presumably not a coincidence.

Hove pressed Manyonda on whether Shava and Bara were not in fact suspended because they held views critical of the government on the investment code issue. Manyonda would not confirm that the two journalists were summoned before the Minister on 19 May but did say:

_____

*   *Zimbabwe: Parliamentary Debates*, May 30, 1989.

**   *Zimbabwe: Parliamentary Debates*, May 31, 1989.

72

All I am aware of is that when we listened to the tapes that involved the interview on Radio 4 we were so perturbed that we brought the situation to the attention of ZBC management. What they did later, quite honestly we do not know.*

According to an unconfirmed report, Shava and Bara were later reinstated and, like Nyarota, promoted out of harm's way.

The exposure of "Willowgate" was an outstanding achievement by the young Zimbabwean press. It was able to occur largely because of the December 1987 unity agreement. The result has been a new era of political openness and a breakdown in traditional party alignments. But now it appears that the opportunity for dissent was only temporary. The *Chronicle* has returned to bland predictability. The *Herald*, under editor Tommy Sithole, continues to ignore financial scandals and to pour scorn on government critics.

In April, after one particularly partial *Herald* report about Edgar Tekere, Judith Todd, a former political prisoner and veteran of the liberation struggle, wrote an open letter to Sithole.

Lack of information and the absence of straightforward reporting are the direct causes of rumour-mongering. A pertinent example of this was the failure of the Herald to report Willowgate until the President announced the appointment of the Sandura Commission of Enquiry. This lack of reporting in the Herald was naturally widely commented on giving rise to the rumour that "Tommy Sithole is himself implicated in Willowgate."...

Without accurate and untarnished information it is difficult for people to make correct decisions and this, at the end of the day, can damage the State....But just as people demand and eventually get a certain standard in the conduct of Government, so people demand and eventually get a certain standard in the press that serves them. That's what the struggle for press freedom is all about.**

---

*   *Ibid.*

**   Letter from Judith Todd to Tommy Sithole, April 29, 1989. The full text appears in Appendix B.

Human rights monitoring

Zimbabwe is unusual in Africa for having a vigorous and independent human rights organization: the Catholic Commission for Justice and Peace in Zimbabwe. A commission of the Zimbabwe Catholic Bishops Conference, it has been monitoring human rights developments since the beginning of the bush war in the early 1970s. The Justice and Peace Commission derives much of its authority from its courageous stand against the Rhodesian Government's abuses, as well as from its political detachment and the accuracy of its information. In 1977 the then chairman of the commission, John Deary, was arrested and charged under the Law and Order (Maintenance) Act, as were three other commission officials: Dieter Scholz, Arthur Dupuis and Janice McLaughlin. Charges were later dropped but Scholz, a Jesuit priest, and McLaughlin, a Maryknoll sister, were both expelled from the country. Pascal Slevin, an Irish Franciscan, was also deported at about the same time for taking photographs of torture victims for publication by the commission.

The clear stand of the Justice and Peace Commission and the Catholic Bishops over the Matabeleland killings has already been cited. In the commission's 1985 annual report, chairman Michael Auret reported on a number of cases of torture: "All reports were investigated and found to be correct, with remarkable similarity in the methods used in all cases." He continued:

> Later in the year Amnesty International reported very similar cases. It is, of course, a great disappointment that the situation in Zimbabwe should call for such a report. I wish to make the point however, that the Commission did not collaborate with Amnesty International in the compiling of evidence or the preparation of the report and that the release of the report was as much a surprise to the Commission as it was to government. The Commission congratulates Amnesty International on the report...*

---

* Catholic Commission for Justice and Peace in Zimbabwe, *Annual Report 1985*, p4.

74

The commission was at pains to distance itself from Amnesty International because of the hostility engendered by an AI report documenting torture in Zimbabwe. The anti-AI campaign, referred to in Chapter 2, culminated in the threat that anyone who supplied information to the human rights organization would be detained. Makhatini Guduza, a UN-recognized refugee in Botswana who was absurdly alleged to be in the pay of Amnesty International, was illegally and forcibly returned to Zimbabwe where he was detained without trial for two years.

In May 1986 the director of the Justice and Peace Commission, Nicholas Ndebele, was arrested and detained under emergency powers regulations, apparently because of alleged connections with Amnesty International. After about two weeks in detention, the High Court ordered his release. Then he was briefly re-detained, along with Michael Auret, before both men were released, apparently on Mugabe's orders.

However, the Justice and Peace Commission continued its work on behalf of detainees and their dependents, as well as bringing the High Court action on behalf of the dependents of "disappeared" people from Silobela, as described in Chapter 3. The commission continues to submit details of its concerns confidentially to government, as well as making public statements on important human rights issues. For example, it was prominent in criticizing the amnesty for human rights violators and the failure to offer a parallel amnesty for those serving sentences for "dissident-related" offenses.

In April 1989 Nicholas Ndebele was detained for 19 hours by the army at Mutandahwe camp in Masvingo province on the Mozambican border, along with Richard Carver of Africa Watch, journalist Karl Maier of the *Independent* and a local teacher. They were arrested when they reported to the army in the border village of Mahenye, where they were seeking information on human rights developments in the conflict with RENAMO. They were repeatedly questioned and at one point threatened with violence. On their return to Harare, Ndebele and Maier were further questioned by police. Carver raised the matter with the Minister of Justice, Legal and Parliamentary Affairs, Emmerson Mnangagwa, who apologized for the army's behavior and advised Africa Watch to raise the matter with the Minister of State for security, Sydney

Sekeramayi, who is also acting Minister of Defence. Mnangagwa said that he was sure that the Minister would order an inquiry into the affair. However, at the time of writing Africa Watch has received no indication from Sekeramayi of any action taken.

Despite these occasional problems, the prestige of the Justice and Peace Commission has usually enabled it to carry out its investigations without official harassment. Zimbabwe now also appears more open to investigations by international human rights organizations. In October 1988 there was a warm official welcome for a "Human Rights Now!" concert sponsored by Amnesty International in Harare and Zimbabwean officials have been ready to respond to Africa Watch's inquiries about detentions and other reported human rights abuses.

Another non-governmental organization, the Legal Resources Foundation, set up in 1985, has been doing important work in making legal services and knowledge of legal rights accessible to a broader public. This has been achieved through publications, legal advice sessions and training programs. In April 1989, the Bulawayo Legal Projects Centre, run by the foundation, began a training program for police and other law enforcement officers in various human rights aspects of criminal procedure.

7. THE CRISIS IN MANICALAND

With the advent of peace in Matabeleland, the situation in Mozambique poses the most serious threat to Zimbabwe's security and to the human rights of Zimbabweans. The threat is caused by the activities of the opposition guerrilla organization RENAMO (Resistencia Nacional Mocambicana — Mozambique National Resistance). RENAMO, which for nearly two decades has waged a brutal war against FRELIMO, the former liberation movement which now forms the government of Mozambique, is now also engaged in frequent attacks on Zimbabwe. However, the cause for concern in the eastern districts of Zimbabwe is not only RENAMO activities, but also the response of the Zimbabwean army. This sharply poses the question of whether the government and army have learnt the lessons of their disastrous mishandling of the Matabeleland crisis.

RENAMO and the Mozambique crisis

RENAMO has always been closely bound up with the internal politics of Zimbabwe. It was formed in the early 1970s by the Rhodesian CIO, primarily as a means of gathering intelligence on the Zimbabwean liberation organizations operating from Mozambique.* In the first instance RENAMO was recruited from among the Ndau, a Shona-related ethnic group which straddles the border between southeastern Zimbabwe and Mozambique. Even today much of the leadership of RENAMO is Ndau, including its top leader, Afonso Dhlakama, and it appears to draw greatest support in Shona-speaking areas of Mozambique. At Zimbabwe's independence in 1980, RENAMO "was

---

*   Flower, *Serving Secretly*, pp300-302 reprints a secret CIO memorandum from 1974 detailing negotiations with Portuguese and South African intelligence about the formation of RENAMO.

transferred lock, stock and barrel" to the South African military.* Under South African control RENAMO rapidly changed from primarily an intelligence organization to one wholly dedicated to sabotage and destabilization. RENAMO's creator Ken Flower later wrote: "I began to wonder whether we had created a monster that was now beyond control."**

In the first three years after Zimbabwean independence the South African military also made at least a dozen direct attacks on Mozambique. These included a raid on the oil tank farm in Beira port by the Reconnaissance Commando in December 1982, which caused a major fuel crisis in Zimbabwe. There were a number of other attacks on Beira and the transport corridor to Zimbabwe, which was the country's main outlet to the sea other than through South Africa. In 1982 Zimbabwe committed a Special Task Force of the national army to guard the Beira-Mutare oil pipeline. The legal basis for the intervention was the 1981 Zimbabwe-Mozambique Defence Agreement. In 1984 Mozambique signed a pact with South Africa at Nkomati, whereby the latter would withdraw its support from RENAMO. However, RENAMO continued to grow in military strength, and Zimbabwean military involvement in Mozambique deepened. In 1985 Zimbabwean paratroopers captured the RENAMO base at "Casa Banana" in Gorongosa. Not only did this signal a deeper Zimbabwean involvement than simply defence of its own strategic interests – Mugabe stated that he was prepared to commit up to 30,000 troops – but it also proved deeply embarrassing to South Africa. At the Gorongosa base the Zimbabwean troops found documents indicating continued South African support for RENAMO in violation of the Nkomati accord, including three visits to Gorongosa by the South Africa deputy foreign minister. RENAMO responded to this increased Zimbabwean involvement by stepping up attacks inside Zimbabwe. In 1986 RENAMO announced that it was "declaring war" on Zimbabwe.

---

*   *Ibid*, pp261-2.

**   *Ibid*, p262.

Human rights abuses by RENAMO

Until recently the Zimbabwean Government has tried to minimize the extent of RENAMO activity within the country, largely for political reasons, since the army's involvement in Mozambique is far from universally popular. Of late, however, it has been more open about RENAMO atrocities, not least because they provide an important rationale for maintaining the state of emergency. In February 1989, introducing the motion in parliament for the renewal of the emergency, Minister of Home Affairs Moven Mahachi cited 420 RENAMO attacks in the preceding six months, with 93 Zimbabwean civilians killed.

RENAMO abuses within Mozambique have been well documented and have received wide international publicity.* The guerrillas have carried out frequent killings, including large-scale massacres, and horrific mutilations of civilians, by cutting off ears, lips, noses and fingers. It is not widely appreciated internationally that RENAMO is perpetrating similar acts in the eastern districts of Zimbabwe. Worst affected are Rushinga and Mount Darwin in the north east and Chipinge, Chiredzi and Chisumbanje in the south east. The following are some of the cases cited by Mahachi to Parliament:

- On August 2, 1988, five RENAMO guerrillas (known as *matsangas*) were seen approaching Wilson Chapu's homestead in Tsovera village, Chiredzi. The villagers fled, leaving behind three children aged between two and five years. The *matsangas* killed the children before looting food and clothing from several homesteads. Occupants of one homestead locked themselves inside a hut. The guerrillas set the hut on fire, although the occupants managed to escape without injury. A woman was abducted and forced to carry the loot, but later escaped.

- Five *matsangas* arrived at Mashamba village, Chiredzi, on August 3, 1988, driving cattle belonging to a local person. They kidnapped two locals, who later escaped unhurt. Twelve people were seriously assaulted with rifle butts and burning wood. One of the 12, Mushava

---

* For example in a report written by Robert Gersony in 1988 for the US State Department. On the basis of interviews with refugees in neighboring countries and displaced people within Mozambique, Gersony estimated that RENAMO had killed some 100,000 civilians.

Lisimati, died on August 4, at Chiredzi hospital from the injuries sustained. The RENAMO members said that they were killing and assaulting villagers because the Zimbabwean army was killing their people in Mozambique.

- RENAMO guerrillas arrived at Chimbi village, Chisumbanje, on August 16, 1988 and opened fire at some local people who were drinking beer. Two died on the spot and three others were injured. As villagers started running away, the *matsangas* bayoneted one woman to death and killed a man by beating him with a pestle. They then looted homesteads and abducted two men, forcing them to carry the loot into Mozambique.

- On September 2, 1988, about six *matsangas* arrived at Ngera village, Rushinga, and found it deserted. The villagers slept at a nearby school under military guard. The guerrillas awaited the return of the villagers. Two elderly women who were the first to arrive back were captured and ordered to go with RENAMO to Mozambique. One refused and was shot dead.

- At Rukangare business center, Chisumbanje, on September 14, 1988, about 10 *matsangas* approached a store owner who was asleep in his house. They demanded money and the keys to the store. He threw them the keys. When he later opened the door, he was struck on the forehead with a machete. The guerrillas stole clothing and groceries and fled into Mozambique.

- On November 29, 1988 about 30 armed RENAMO members arrived at Ndali village in Chiredzi communal lands, where they surrounded local people who were buying meat. They bayoneted seven of them to death, including a one-year-old child, and seriously injured three others. They looted clothing and food and abducted two local people whom they forced to carry off the loot. Two days later, in Gona-re-Zhou National Park, one of those abducted escaped, but the other was bayoneted to death. The dead were identified as Mafanda Mataiwa, Hlengani Mataiwa, Fransina Bhujule, Juliet Hlongwani, Innocent Sibanda, Kiyasi Hlahungazi, Mupagati Sinbanda and an unnamed woman, aged 54 years.

- At Kashava village, under Chief Chigango, in Mount Darwin area, on December 4, 1988, about seven *matsangas* arrived at Kashere Kamros's homestead. They fired indiscriminately at the family sitting outside their huts. Kamros was shot and died later; the rest of the family was unhurt. The RENAMO members looted homesteads and burned a hut, before fleeing across the border.*

Political opposition in Manicaland

These abuses are the responsibility not only of RENAMO, but of the Government of South Africa which has armed and trained the *matsangas* since 1980, in a *contra*-style operation. However, in addition to the security problems posed by RENAMO, these operations also present the Zimbabwean Government with a considerable political headache. Since the Special Task Force was first committed to Mozambique there has been domestic Zimbabwean opposition to the military entanglement. At first this came mainly from ZAPU, partly because it was alleged that former ZIPRA troops were being pushed into the front line and suffering heavier casualties. Of late opposition to Zimbabwe's military involvement in Mozambique has grown, especially in the eastern areas which have borne the brunt of RENAMO's revenge attacks. (Note the explicit link made by the *matsangas* who killed Mushava Lisimati at Mashamba village in August 1988 between their attack and the role of the Zimbabwean army in Mozambique.) Since ZUM was formed in April 1988, a prominent part of its platform has been military withdrawal from Mozambique. ZUM's leader, Edgar Tekere, is from the eastern border province of Manicaland and is clearly articulating a sentiment that he knows to be popular in his home area.

Opposition is also likely to be considerable among the Ndau who live in the Chipinge area on the Zimbabwean side of the border, because of their ethnic affinity with many of the *matsangas*. In the 1985 general election Chipinge was the only constituency in a Shona-speaking area of the country to return a member of parliament who was not a member of ZANU-PF. He is Goodson Sithole, of the party ZANU-*Ndonga* which is led from exile by Reverend Ndabaningi Sithole.** The government has repeatedly accused Reverend

---

*   *Zimbabwe: Parliamentary Debates*, January 24, 1989.

**   In May 1989 Goodson Sithole was arrested in connection with unpaid debts, according to a police spokesperson. *Ndonga* means walking stick - the party's electoral symbol - and is used to distinguish it from ZANU-PF. The two parties split in the 1970s.

Sithole of being in league with RENAMO. It must seriously fear that the people of Chipinge not only oppose Zimbabwe's military involvement in Mozambique, but may in some instances have more enthusiasm for RENAMO than for their own government.

The political situation in eastern Zimbabwe is further complicated by one of the great unresolved issues since independence: land. The importance of the land issue in the struggle for independence was referred to in Chapter 1. However, since 1980 there has been no reform of the system of land tenure, nor a radical redistribution of land from the large-scale commercial farms to the land-hungry peasants in the communal areas. Manicaland is the area of the country where that pressure has been most acute. When Africa Watch's delegate visited Zimbabwe in April 1989, he saw an èxample of the discontent caused by the land problem on a farm in the Cashel valley in Manicaland. Some 21 families (about 200 people) were camped there in squalid conditions – and in some danger of attack from RENAMO – after being evicted from land in nearby Chimanimani. They constituted only about a quarter of the families evicted from two farms, Hangani and Sawerombi. The families from Hangani had owned the land before it had been taken by white settlers in the 1890s. They had been allowed to stay on the land as farm laborers until late 1988 when they were evicted under a court order obtained by the present owner. The other farm, Sawerombi, had been abandoned by the white owner shortly after independence and families from the neighboring communal areas had moved on to the land and farmed it as a cooperative. In 1987 the same owner acquired the land. It appears that the land has been bought for speculative purposes rather than productive use; after independence this same farmer bought a number of farms in Cashel which he resold to the government and Forestry Commission for a considerable profit in 1983. The Sawerombi "squatters" were also evicted in late 1988.*

It is apparent that in Manicaland there is the same explosive cocktail of destabilizing factors which led to such serious insecurity in Matabeleland:

---

*   The full story of the Hangani and Sawerombi evictions is told in *Moto*, No 77, June 1989.

armed insurgency, organized political opposition and social grievances. What is most disturbing is that the government appears to be reacting in precisely the same manner to the RENAMO threat as it did to the "dissidents" in Matabeleland. Instead of making a clear distinction between legitimate political dissent and armed opposition, it is amalgamating ZUM, RENAMO and South Africa, in precisely the same manner as it did in Matabeleland. If legal avenues of political opposition are closed, it is not inconceivable that popular support for RENAMO will grow.

To combat RENAMO the army in the border areas has revived an old tactic from the Smith years: the protected village. In all the areas worst affected by RENAMO attacks the civilian population is compelled to gather together at night under army protection. In some areas, however, local people have complained that the protection provided is inadequate — in Rushinga it is complained that in four years the army has failed to engage RENAMO. Some observers comment that the main purpose of the protected village policy is to separate Zimbabweans from Mozambican refugees and migrants.

The treatment of Mozambican refugees

Historically there have been large numbers of Mozambican migrant workers in eastern Zimbabwe, particularly on the large farms and the tea and sugar plantations. In recent years these numbers have been swelled by refugees fleeing the political violence in Mozambique. Official figures put the number of refugees in camps at 75,000, with some 100,000 spontaneously settled elsewhere. Mozambicans in Zimbabwe have borne the brunt of the government's frustration at its inability to deter RENAMO attacks. According to refugee organizations, between 8,000 and 9,000 Mozambicans were illegally and summarily expelled from Zimbabwe in 1988, usually on the allegation that they were RENAMO supporters and often in direct response to a particular RENAMO attack. In fact expelled refugees have usually ended up in reception centers run by the Mozambican Government — suggesting that they were not RENAMO supporters. Refugee organizations say that the Zimbabwean authorities have moderated their behavior towards Mozambican refugees and that there have been fewer expulsions in 1989. However, they also comment that there is often

83

a considerable gap between the enlightened attitude of the civilian authorities and the behavior of the army on the ground. Clearly Mozambicans in Zimbabwe outside the refugee camps remain at risk.*

Africa Watch has also come across disturbing evidence of abuse by the Zimbabwean army against Mozambicans within their own country. Africa Watch has asked the Zimbabwe Government to conduct an urgent inquiry into the detention of about 35 Mozambicans, including small children, arrested in Espungabera on March 16, 1989. Those detained included the families of Pio Mutambara and Edmore Simango. In mid-April they were held by the Grey's Scouts in Mutandahwe camp, inside Zimbabwe.** They alleged that they had been tortured, a claim which was given substance by the fact that one of those detained had clearly suffered serious damage to his legs. They said that they expected to be transferred to Tongogara refugee camp, which suggests that they were not seriously suspected of being in contact with RENAMO.

Africa Watch has received no reply to its inquiries about these prisoners. A number of informants have told Africa Watch that the Zimbabwean army is deliberately depopulating a wide swathe of territory down the Mozambican side of the border and that many of those removed from their villages have been imprisoned inside Zimbabwe. Such claims are, by their nature, difficult to confirm. However, the case of the prisoners at Mutandhawe suggests that in at least one instance the allegation has substance.

---

*   Zimbabwe also has a poor record for seeking the illegal repatriation of refugees from neighboring countries. The case of Makhatini Guduza, who was forcibly returned in 1986 and then detained without trial for two years was described in Chapter 6. Leslie Lesia was illegally deported from Mozambique to Zimbabwe in 1987 (see Chapter 4). Earlier in 1983 and 1984, possibly as many as dozens of Zimbabwean refugees from Matabeleland were illegally returned from Botswana, many of whom were then detained for long periods and, in some instances, tortured. More recently, in 1988, Dennis Charles Beahan was illegally returned from Botswana to Zimbabwe where he was wanted for his alleged involvement in a plan to rescue a group of South African saboteurs from prison. He claims that he was tortured while in custody in Botswana. In June 1989 Beahan was found guilty and sentenced to life imprisonment by the High Court in Harare.

**   It was here that they were seen by Africa Watch's delegate, who was temporarily held by the Grey's Scouts. See page 58.

8. AFRICA WATCH'S RECOMMENDATIONS

This report is published at the present time because now is something of a watershed in Zimbabwean history. With the advent of unity between ZANU-PF and ZAPU the period of the worst human rights abuses is over. However, the emergence of a new political party with a degree of popular support is straining the government's adherence to freedom of political association and throwing into question its planned moves towards a single-party system. Next year, 1990, the government will have much greater freedom to amend the constitution handed to Zimbabwe at independence nearly 10 years ago. Also the first moves towards peace talks between the warring parties in Mozambique hold out the promise of greater security on the eastern border. President Mugabe is playing a leading role as mediator in these negotiations. Potentially, therefore, the next few months could be a period of important political and constitutional development. Africa Watch hopes that they might be a time to consolidate various safeguards against human rights abuse in the future, if the lessons of recent years can be learnt. In this chapter we summarize Africa Watch's recommendations to the Zimbabwean Government for measures to safeguard against human rights abuse.

Punishment of human rights violators

The importance of bringing human rights violators to justice is that this is a declaration that no one is above the law, not even the most powerful members of the state apparatus. For this reason the obligation on the authorities to bring charges against those believed to have committed human rights abuse is even greater than when similar crimes are committed by ordinary citizens. Unfortunately, by means of indemnity regulations, amnesties and simple failure to prosecute, the Zimbabwean Government has instead created the impression that certain agencies — notably the CIO, but on occasions branches of the police and army too — are a law unto themselves.

85

The retention of torturers and other human rights violators in positions of authority and the failure to take action against them unmistakably suggest that the government does not regard such crimes as serious. They also greatly increase the likelihood that human rights violations will recur. The government's failure to take action against human rights violators also discourages individuals from complaining about abuses for fear that they will be further victimized.

The Zimbabwean Government has been criticized for failing to amnesty civilians imprisoned for "dissident" offenses, when it has released members of security forces who have committed similar, or often more serious, crimes. This inconsistency reinforces the impression that members of the security forces and ruling party are not subject to the rule of law. Africa Watch urges the government to release all those serving sentences for "dissident" offenses under a general amnesty. We also urge that there be no future general amnesties for those responsible for human rights abuses and that the government's intention to prosecute those of its servants who abuse human rights be clearly and publicly stated.

Africa Watch also urges the government to repeal the Protection of Wildlife (Indemnity) Act, passed earlier this year, which protects game wardens from prosecution for abuses. We consider this likely to encourage such abuses, as well as being contrary to the basic principle of equality before the law.

Payment of compensation

Payment of compensation is one of the most important remedies when an individual's rights are violated by agents of the state. The right to seek redress through the courts is guaranteed in international human rights instruments. Yet, despite several rulings by Zimbabwean courts in favor of victims of abuse, the government has apparently never paid compensation. As detailed in Chapter 3, this appears to be a matter of deliberate government policy.

Africa Watch urges the Zimbabwean Government to alter its practice in this regard and to make compensation payments to victims of human rights abuse, including unlawful detention and torture, as well as to the relatives of people who have "disappeared" or been victims of political killings by members of the security forces. Such payments should be made without prejudice to any other criminal or civil proceedings.

Investigation of complaints

A precondition to both the prosecution of human rights violators and the payment of compensation to those whose rights have been abused is the prompt and impartial investigation of allegations of abuse. Under its Commissions of Inquiry Act Zimbabwe has the mechanism to conduct major investigations with most of the necessary guarantees of impartiality. Its major weakness is that it does not require investigations to be conducted publicly or to publish their conclusion. Thus, for example, a major commission of inquiry on human rights abuses in Matabeleland in 1983 reported to the government but its findings have never been made public. Although human rights investigations may occasionally have to proceed in private, the general rule should be that they are public in order to safeguard their impartiality.

Two issues are in particular need of urgent inquiry. One is the still unresolved question of "disappearances," both of prisoners held in police custody and of people abducted in rural areas of Matabeleland and Midlands, apparently by the security forces (see Chapter 3). The aim of such an investigation would be to determine their whereabouts, to enable death certificates to be issued where appropriate, to facilitate the payment of compensation to their relatives and to prepare for criminal prosecution of those responsible for the "disappearances."

The second issue which needs investigation is the continuing use of torture, particularly by the CIO (see Chapter 5). The aim of such an investigation would be to establish the truth of continuing allegations of torture, to facilitate the payment of compensation to those who have been tortured and to prepare criminal prosecutions of those law enforcement officials alleged to have carried out torture. Pending criminal proceedings they should be removed from their posts.

In addition there should be a permanent mechanism whereby individual complaints of abuse can be investigated. By this means a person who alleges that he or she has been tortured or that a relative has "disappeared" can

87

have his or her complaint promptly and impartially investigated. This might be achieved, for example, by expanding the existing office of the Ombudsman, who looks into complaints of maladministration. However, such a body should also have the discretion to initiate inquiries when there has been no complaint, since there are many reasons why people who have suffered traumatic experiences such as torture may be reluctant to come forward to present their complaint.

Human rights training

An important safeguard against human rights abuse is to train law enforcement officials in proper standards. There have already been important steps in this regard: for example the instructions issued to the police in 1986 forbidding torture and the training courses for law enforcement officers run the Bulawayo Legal Projects Centre. It is important that such educational initiatives be extended to all those involved in law enforcement and custody of prisoners.

State of Emergency and detention without trial

Zimbabwe has been governed under a State of Emergency since 1965. The principal aim in maintaining the emergency seems to be to allow the use of detention without trial under the Emergency Powers (Maintenance of Law and Order) Regulations. However, as documented in this report, the ostensible reason for maintaining the emergency is the security situation in Manicaland, yet none of those detained has had any connection with the insecurity on the eastern border. Also an increasing proportion of those detained have continued to be held after the Detainees' Review Tribunal has recommended their release. Africa Watch believes that the time has come for the State of Emergency to be lifted, in order to allow the unhindered enjoyment of the liberties set out in Zimbabwe's Declaration of Rights.

Africa Watch recommends that the government should not retain any powers to detain indefinitely without trial, though it does recognize that in situations of insecurity it may be necessary to detain for longer than the 48-hour period stipulated in the Criminal Procedure and Evidence Act. However, it is important that there is a time limit on detention without charge which is strictly observed. It is also essential that the government abides by the recommendations of its own Review Tribunal, which provides the only adjudication as to whether there is good reason for a person to be detained.

Independence of the judiciary

As noted in this report, Zimbabwe's formal record since independence in respecting the independence of the judiciary has been good (Chapter 4). However, in two areas the government has intervened to undermine judicial decisions. One is by detaining people who have been acquitted by the courts or, more often in recent months, charging people frivolously, withdrawing charges before they go to court and then detaining them. Detention powers are for use only in extreme cases of insecurity where normal investigatory procedures are delayed. In Zimbabwe they have been used in an arbitrary manner which interferes with the independence of the courts and the right to liberty of the individual.

The second interference in judicial independence has been the use of pardons for those convicted by the courts. Thus Robert Masikini of the CIO was released only a week after being sentenced to death for murdering a prisoner and former minister Frederick Shava was not required to serve a prison sentence imposed for lying to a judicial inquiry.

The sum of all this must be a decline in respect for the impartiality of the law. If you are a law enforcement officer or a political functionary you can be released even if a court sends you to prison. If you are a political critic or member of an ethnic minority you can go to prison even if the court acquits you. Africa Watch believes that the Zimbabwe Government understands the importance of an independent judicial system in the protection of human rights and urges it to end these abuses.

Freedom of speech

To a large extent freedom of speech is safeguarded by the absence of state reprisals against those who wish to criticize. The abolition of detention without trial and a serious drive to eliminate torture would thus be the most important measures in this regard.

However, the prospects for free discussion in the press would be much improved if the government were prepared to loosen its control on the country's main newspapers. In particular the Ministry of Information should stop its direct intervention in the running of newspapers and broadcasting, for example to discipline journalists of whom it disapproves (Chapter 6). Editorial freedom might be best protected by broadening the ownership of main newspapers and encouraging active participation by different individuals and organizations in the Mass Media Trust.

Freedom of association

Although Zimbabwe remains a multi-party state, in practice the government has been highly intolerant of organized dissent (Chapter 6). The unfortunate effect of this has been to drive peaceful critics into the arms of those who seek to undermine Zimbabwe's security. The treatment of the new Zimbabwe Unity Movement — meetings banned and officials arrested — does not bode well for the future of multi-party politics in Zimbabwe. Africa Watch urges the government to ensure that this harassment of ZUM does not continue and that the new party is free to canvas peacefully for popular support. This also means that the ruling party should restrain its own members, particularly the Youth and Women's Leagues, from acts of harassment and violence against supporters of minority groups.

President Mugabe's repeated assurances that a one-party political system will not be imposed against the wishes of the majority are welcome. However, it would be helpful if the government were to state how precisely it intends to gauge the popular will on this issue, given that the one-party state remains its long-term objective.

Labor rights

Africa Watch recommends the repeal of the State of Emergency, which would mean that the recently enacted Emergency Powers (Maintenance of

Essential Services) Regulations would become void. These make strikes in essential services illegal. Africa Watch recommends repeal of other legislation outlawing strikes, particularly the relevant sections of the Law and Order (Maintenance) Act and the Labor Relations Act, and the withdrawal of any charges currently pending under these laws.

It is not unreasonable for the government to retain the power to protect the running of essential services in times of extreme emergency, such as war. However, it is important that such a power is not abused by being kept in force permanently. It is also important, if the right to strike is to have any meaning, that "essential services" are defined more narrowly than at present. Africa Watch urges the repeal of Rhodesia Government Notice 798(A) of 1965, which extends the definition to all finance, commerce and industry.

The rights of refugees

The community of Mozambican refugees and exiles is the most vulnerable in Zimbabwe, with no one to articulate their concerns and with the permanent fear of returning to their troubled homeland. The presence of many tens of thousands of refugees has undoubtedly put a considerable strain on the government's resources, but the response of the Zimbabwean authorities has often been found wanting. The expulsion of some 8-9,000 Mozambicans in 1988 exposed them to the very abuses they had fled Mozambique to escape. There appears to have been no serious procedure to investigate and verify the broad allegation that those expelled were RENAMO supporters. Fewer Mozambicans appear to have been expelled in 1989, but there is clearly still a need for the government to review its policy and practice towards refugees to ensure that these are in line with its legal obligations under the UN Convention Relating to the Status of Refugees and the OAU Convention Governing the Specific Aspects of Refugee Problems in Africa.

The Zimbabwean Government has assured Africa Watch that there would be a full investigation of an incident in March 1989 involving the arrest and alleged torture of a group of Mozambicans, abducted from their village in Mozambique and held in an army camp inside Zimbabwe (Chapter 7). We have not been informed of the results of any such inquiry and would urge that all reported instances of abuses by the army in Mozambique and eastern Zimbabwe be fully and promptly investigated.

International human rights instruments

Although it ratified the African Charter on Human and Peoples' Rights in 1986, Zimbabwe is not party to any of the major United Nations human rights instruments. Africa Watch urges the Zimbabwean Government to begin moves to ratify the International Covenant on Civil and Political Rights (with its Optional Protocol) and the Convention Against Torture or Other Cruel, Inhuman or Degrading Treatment or Punishment. Not only do these treaties give legal force to the rights first codified in the Universal Declaration of Human Rights (of which the Zimbabwean Government has declared itself a staunch supporter); they also incorporate mechanisms for reviewing the adherence of states to the provisions of the treaties and investigating complaints from individuals who claim that their rights have been violated.

9. UNITED STATES POLICY

Relations between the United States and independent Zimbabwe have frequently been strained. Successive Secretaries of State played an important role in the negotiations which led to independence in 1980, promising a multi-million dollar fund to pay for land bought for resettlement — one historian later referred to the "fog of half promises that Britain and the US would pick up the bill."* In the event the US has contributed no funds directly for resettlement.**

In many respects its proximity to South Africa has been Zimbabwe's misfortune — not least because non-African countries seem incapable of judging Zimbabwe on its own merits rather than as part of a regional game plan. In May 1984 the then Deputy Assistant Secretary of State for African Affairs, Frank Wisner, testified before the Africa Sub-Committee of the Congressional Foreign Affairs Committee. He stated the Reagan Administration's doctrine towards Zimbabwe in terms that probably approximate to present thinking:

> In the 4 years of its independence, Zimbabwe has captured the interest of many Americans. It is only right that it should. Zimbabwe's coming to independence — via the 1979 negotiations at Lancaster House between the British Government and the Zimbabwean parties — was a triumph of diplomacy and one in which the US played an important supporting role.
>
> We have watched Zimbabwe emerge from a bloody civil war and begin the construction of a new nation, committed to national reconciliation, non-racialism, democratic

---

*   Quoted in *Moto*, No 77, June 1989.

**   *Ibid.* Britain has provided only about 10 per cent of the US$500 million estimated as necessary to buy land to resettle 165,000 families.

procedures, the rule of law, social justice, and economic development.

There have been no war crime trials.*

We are to infer, presumably, that the rule of law is best served by *failing* to prosecute those responsible for war crimes or other human rights violations. At the time of this testimony, in May 1984, for the second year running the Zimbabwean army had just conducted a brutal suppression of the population of Matabeleland. The human rights abuses involved in this operation were already well-documented. Yet Wisner did not feel the need to modify his comments about national reconciliation and the rule of law ("We appreciate the fact that the Government of Zimbabwe has taken action to rectify conditions which have led to the violations of basic human rights."). Clearly there were other more important considerations:

> Zimbabwe inherited a reasonably strong economy, with an active private sector. While buffeted heavily by world recession, transportation difficulties, drought, and a certain amount of Socialist rhetoric, it has been managed by the new leadership with a respect of market principles and international economic realities and in cooperation with international economic institutions...Flatly stated, Zimbabwe is critical to our policy in Southern Africa...**

Given such enthusiasm for Zimbabwe's political and economic direction, it is perhaps curious that the Reagan Administration should have felt the need to cut aid to Zimbabwe for reasons ostensibly unconnected with the situation in southern Africa.*** At the time Zimbabwe was a member of the UN Security Council, in which capacity it abstained on a resolution condemning the Soviet Union for shooting down the Korean airliner, flight KAL 007, and cosponsored a resolution condemning the US invasion of Grenada.

---

*   Hearing before the Subcommittee on Africa of the Committee in Foreign Affairs, House of Representatives, May 24, 1984.

**   *Ibid.*

***   The US reduced its aid under ZIMCORD (Zimbabwe Conference on Reconstruction and Development) from $35 million in fiscal year 1984 to $30 million in FY 1985.

Then, in July 1986, the Reagan Administration froze all aid after a Zimbabwean Minister had chosen a July 4 reception in Harare, attended by former President Jimmy Carter, as the occasion for a major attack on US policy in southern Africa. Prime Minister Mugabe responded in the following terms:

> This is the behaviour of a country which in one vein would want us to believe that it does not ever want to impose sanctions (against South Africa) and in another it is imposing sanctions against us for saying it refused to impose sanctions against South Africa. I find that quite ironical...*

Mugabe's irritation and irony is understandable. A tactless speech at a social function is apparently deemed to be more blameworthy than the systematic denial of human rights to millions of black South Africans. A further irony — though clearly Mugabe was not going to mention this — is that the years 1983-86, when aid was first cut and then frozen, were the period of the worst human rights violations in post-independence Zimbabwe, yet the United States imposed its sanctions for different and essentially trivial reasons. This is regrettable not only because of any ill effects on Zimbabwe itself, but also because it leaves the present administration with little moral authority to exert with the Zimbabwean Government over human rights issues.

In August 1988 aid was unfrozen when the Reagan Administration signed a US$17 million grant to the Zimbabwean Government. Commenting on the resumption of the aid program, US Ambassador James Rawlings attached importance to: "The recognition that Zimbabwe's economy is healthy and dynamic with the potential for greater growth based on the successes of the past." Since then Zimbabwe has won further foreign approval with its new investment package, unveiled in May 1989, which includes opening negotiations to sign the US Overseas Private Investment Corporation (OPIC) agreement. At the same time as the $17 million grant, about $200,000 was provided under the International Military Education and Training (IMET) program for training in the US.

---

*   *Zimbabwe: Parliamentary Debates*, July 16, 1986, cited in Ibbo Mandaza "The Post-White Settler Colonial Situation" in Mandaza (ed), *Zimbabwe: the Political Economy of Transition 1980-1986*, CODESRIA, 1987.

Apart from the resumption of aid, there are other factors which suggest that the administration may have greater leverage in Harare than in the past. One is the administration's commendably unequivocal condemnation of atrocities by RENAMO. The other is the evolution of the peace process in Angola, where US aid to the South African-backed rebels of Jonas Savimbi's UNITA has been a major stumbling block in relations with Zimbabwe and other southern African front-line states.*

Africa Watch hopes that the administration will use any such leverage to persuade the Zimbabwean Government to use the present period of relative political calm and openness to conduct a full investigation of past abuses and to introduce institutional safeguards to provide greater guarantees of freedom of speech and freedom from arbitrary arrest and torture.

---

*   This is discussed in detail in an April 1989 Africa Watch report *Angola: Violations of the Laws of War by Both Sides*, pp109-17. In the report, which documented extensive human rights violations by UNITA, Africa Watch called on the Bush Administration to withdraw assistance from the rebel movement.

APPENDIX A

Correspondence between Africa Watch and Hon. Moven Mahachi MP, Minister of Home Affairs

1. Africa Watch to Minister Mahachi, May 4, 1989

Dear Minister,

I am writing on behalf of Africa Watch, a committee of Human Rights Watch, which monitors human rights practices and promotes respect for internationally recognized standards. Human Rights Watch also comprises Americas Watch, Asia Watch and Helsinki Watch. Since it was established in May 1988, Africa Watch has undertaken work on a number of countries, including South Africa, Somalia, Sudan, Kenya, Liberia, Angola and Malawi.

I was visiting Harare last week, where I contacted your Ministry to try to arrange an appointment, although unfortunately it was not possible to find a mutually convenient time. However, I was able to meet your colleague, the Minister of Justice, Legal and Parliamentary Affairs, Cde Emmerson Mnangagwa. We discussed matters of mutual concern, including the continued imprisonment of a number of detainees whose release had been recommended by the Detainees' Review Tribunal. Cde Mnangagwa suggested that I write to you about this matter.

Africa Watch is concerned about the growing number of cases in which the President has used his authority to overrule recommendations by the Review Tribunal that a detainee should be released. It is our understanding that from independence until 1985 this power was not invoked, but since then it has been used increasingly. We do not consider that the Review Tribunal, which is a government-appointed administrative tribunal meeting in camera, constitutes a suitably impartial body for reviewing the cases of Zimbabwean citizens deprived of their liberty. However, if properly used, it can provide a safeguard against the worst abuses of administrative detention. When its recommendations are repeatedly overruled or disregarded, the effectiveness of the tribunal is diminished.

Africa Watch urges the release of a number of detainees, all of whom have received favourable Review Tribunal recommendations:

John Lewis-Walker, a senior civil servant, was arrested in September 1987 and detained under the Emergency Powers (Maintenance of Law and Order) Regulations. The Review Tribunal recommended his release in early 1988, but the President overruled this. Lewis-Walker was then charged with espionage, although this charge was withdrawn in August 1988 and he was issued with a new detention order. The Review Tribunal recommended his release for a second time and again this recommendation was overruled. We understand that since then a further favourable tribunal decision has been overruled and that he remains in detention at Chikurubi Maximum Prison.

Patricia Brown was one of a group of six people, including John Lewis-Walker, arrested in September 1987. The broad outlines of her case are the same as Lewis-Walker's. A Review Tribunal decision in favour of her release was rejected in october 1988. She remains at Chikurubi, where she is reported to be in a poor mental state as a consequence of her detention.

Joseph Muchakuchi, aged 19 or 20, was arrested in January 1988. He is the nephew of Philip Conjwayo, who was convicted of murder for his part in the Trenance bombing in Bulawayo on behalf of the South African Government. It is believed that the allegation against Muchakuchi is that he acted as a courier for his uncle. However, the Review Tribunal has recommended his release and Africa watch is concerned that the only reason for his continuing detention is his family relationship to Conjwayo.

Terence and Gail Downey were arrested in July 1988, apparently on the allegation that they were involved in a plan to rescue Gail Downey's brother, Michael Smith, from Chikurubi where he was on remand on charges arising from the Trenance bombing and other alleged acts of violence on behalf of South Africa. However, we understand that the review Tribunal has subsequently recommended their release and we urge the government to comply with that decision.

Finally, Africa Watch is also concerned about the case of Leslie Johannes Lesia, a South African national arrested in Mozambique in April or May 1987 and handed over, apparently without legal basis, to the Zimbabwean authorities. Lesia is alleged to have been so badly beaten by the Central Intelligence Organization at Goromonzi detention centre that both his legs were broken. Charges against him in connection with a bomb explosion in Harare in May 1987 were dropped in October 1988, but he remains in detention under emergency powers. We are not aware that the Review Tribunal has yet considered his case. If this is so, then Leslie Lesia has been imprisoned for two years without the grounds for his imprisonment having been reviewed by any competent tribunal, whether judicial or administrative.

We should stress that in none of these cases does Africa Watch seek to condone acts of sabotage or espionage, nor to minimize the very real threat to Zimbabwe's security posed by the South African Government and military apparatus. However, in each of these cases the detaining authority has not convinced an administrative tribunal sitting in camera that there are sufficient grounds to deprive the individual concerned of his or her liberty. We urge you therefore to conduct an immediate personal review of these cases, with a view to releasing these prisoners unconditionally.

We look forward to learning of your response to our concerns, whether directly or through the Zimbabwean High Commissioner in London, Dr Herbert Murerwa, to whom I am copying this letter.

Yours sincerely,

Richard Carver
Research Director, Africa Watch

2. Minister Mahachi to Africa Watch, June 19, 1989

Dear Sir,

Re: MONITOR ON HUMAN RIGHTS PRACTICES

I acknowledge with thanks receipt of your letter addressed to me dated May 4, 1989 regarding Africa watch's concerns on human rights.

I was sorry to read that on your visit to Harare around the last week of April,1989, you tried to arrange a meeting with me, but regrettably the meeting failed. It is not normally my practice not to see people who may have indicated an interest to meet me for the purpose of exchanging ideas on matters of mutual interest. I, however, feel happy that at least you managed to meet my colleague — the Minister of Justice, Legal and Parliamentary Affairs.

In your letter you stated that "Africa Watch" is concerned about the growing number of cases in which the President has used his authority to overrule recommendations by the Review Tribunal that a detainee should be released.

Whilst I know it is your right to criticise us, I do not appreciate your concerns over imagined Human Rights violations. Human rights implies observance and respect of the law governing the rights and duties of men in society. If any person chooses to blatantly abuse human rights by working for the destabilisation of our sovereign State, we, as a people have no choice but to deal with whoever is involved according to the law of Zimbabwe and nobody has a right to tell us how to react.

Thus Solus [sic] populi suprema lex is the fundamental law for our operation within the territorial realm of Zimbabwe. We reserve the right to take any appropriate action that we consider adequate to meet any challenge in order to guarantee the security of our sovereignity [sic] as a people.

In view of the above submission, I am sure you will appreciate our stand and avoid meddling in our internal affairs.

I hope the foregoing is worthwhile advice for you on all matters internal to Zimbabwe.

Yours sincerely,

M E Mahachi, MP.
Minister of Home Affairs

3. Africa Watch to Minister Mahachi, July 17, 1989

Dear Minister,

Thank you for your letter of June 19, 1989 in reply to mine of May 4. I am grateful to you for taking the time to reply to Africa Watch's concerns.

Africa Watch agrees wholeheartedly that foreign destabilization of the sovereign state of Zimbabwe is a violation of the human rights of Zimbabweans and attempt to undermine your country's hard-won independence. You will have noted that my letter of May 4 stated that Africa Watch did not "condone acts of sabotage or espionage," nor seek to "minimize the very real threat to Zimbabwe's security posed by the South African Government and military apparatus." You may also be interested to know that in April 1989 Africa Watch published a major report on Angola in which we called on the United States Administration to stop its support for the war of destabilization waged by UNITA, because of serious human rights violations by the latter.

However, in the cases cited in my letter, the point at issue is a different one. Not only have these detainees not been convicted in a court of law, but the allegations against them have not even been sustained by the government's own administrative Review Tribunal considering their cases *in camera*. If there is indeed evidence that these are people who "blatantly abuse human rights by working for the destabilisation of our sovereign State," one would expect that evidence of such wrongdoing would have been presented to the Review Tribunal. By recommending their release, the tribunal has said that it finds such evidence somewhat less than compelling.

We appreciate your acknowledgment that it is "your right to criticize us," though I note also that you accuse Africa Watch of "meddling in our internal affairs." It is certainly not our intention to subvert Zimbabwe's sovereignty. Human rights instruments, such as the African Charter on Human and Peoples' Rights to which Zimbabwe is party, proclaim the protection of human rights to be an international responsibility. Our concern is that the detention of prisoners after the Review Tribunal has recommended their release violates the provisions of that Charter guarding against arbitrary detention, as well as similar provisions in the Universal Declaration of Human Rights.

Because of its precarious position and the frequent threats to its sovereignty, Zimbabwe deserves widespread sympathy and solidarity. However, the detention of individuals without credible evidence of their wrongdoing is only likely to undermine the international support that Zimbabwe enjoys.

Africa Watch urges you once again to conduct an immediate personal review of the cases of John Lewis-Walker, Patricia Brown, Joseph Mujakati, Terence and Gail Downey and Leslie Lesia, with a view to their unconditional release.

I thank you again for your attention to this matter.

Yours sincerely,

Richard Carver
Research Director

4. Minister Mahachi to Africa Watch, August 9, 1989

Dear Mr Carver,

In response to your letter of July 17, 1989, I can rest assure you the detainees in question will not be unnecessary held for no good reasons.

As soon as we are convinced that they no longer posed a threat to our security or the information they have or they were collecting is no longer of any use to our potential enemies, they will be released.

Yours sincerely,

Hon M E Mahachi, M.P.
MINISTER OF HOME AFFAIRS

APPENDIX B

Open letter from Judith Todd to Tommy Sithole, editor of the Herald, April 29 1989

Dear Comrade Sithole,

AN OPEN LETTER

This letter is sparked by the front page report in the Herald last Wednesday (April 26) "TEKERE AND CAZ MEMBERS FORM NEW PARTY" which made me think the time was ripe to draw your attention to and invite your comments on some of the important issues confronting the press in Zimbabwe today.

1. Background

People in this country have always been intensely interested in news, even when they haven't had much formal access to it, and even when authorities have tried to suppress information. An outstanding example of this was over the attempted settlement between "Rhodesia" and Britain and the subsequent Pearce Commission, 1971 and 1972. By that time the ANC had been banned, the NDP had been banned, ZAPU had been banned and then on that dramatic day in August 1964 PCC, ZANU and the African Daily News were all banned in one fell swoop. Just before UDI crushingly repressive regulations were imposed under the state of emergency, all news emanating within the country was censored and often distorted and there weren't many avenues of communication left to carry news to the population, particularly in the rural areas. Despite all this people gathered news, fed each other information and thus were able to rally together in that massive NO throughout the country to the Smith-Home proposals.

2. Independence

Eventually came Independence and the buying out of South African interests in our press through the newly established Mass Media Trust (MMT). Freedom of conscience, of expression and association were enshrined in the justiciable Declaration of Rights of the Zimbabwe Constitution where freedom of expression is defined as "the freedom to hold opinions and to receive and impart ideas and information without interference." In retrospect, however, it is difficult to say that our freedom of expression has not been interfered with since Independence as, over the years, Government seems to have had a hand in the sacking of editors employed by Zimbabwe Newspapers (Zimpapers) leading, I am sure, to a sense of great insecurity for someone in your position. This may be the reason why when outrages in our country sometimes occurred, as they did, there was not a professional response from our press. It must be conceded, though, that there can never be any true freedom of the press while we still live under emergency regulations first declared in November 1965 to facilitate Smith's illegal declaration of independence, and maintained for other reasons during and after Zimbabwe's legitimate attainment of Independence.

3. Rumours

The years up to Willowgate can be characterised in the Zimpapers' stable as being on the whole that of obsequiousness to the chefs. But that time has gone. Welcome or not there is now a new relationship discernible between the press and the people. The widely expressed resentment regarding Cde Nyarota's "promotion" shows that those concerned with the press can no longer ride roughshod over the people in attempting to placate the chefs.

The day you published the report mentioned above I thought there must have been a complete breakdown of buses in central Harare. But no, people were queuing in their hundreds simply to buy the newspaper. They knew that Cde Tekere might be up to something and they wanted to know it, even if their own powers of deduction were required to sift what few grains of fact were discernible in the report.

106

It's reports like this that give rise to the extremely high rate of speculation and rumour there is, particularly within Harare. Lack of information and the absence of straightforward reporting are the direct causes of rumour-mongering. A pertinent example of this was the failure of the Herald to report Willowgate until the President announced the appointment of the Sandura Commission of Enquiry. This lack of reporting in the Herald was naturally widely commented on giving rise to the rumour that "Tommy Sithole himself is implicated in Willowgate".

4. Unhealthy and potentially dangerous situation

The months before us are of crucial importance leading through congresses to the elections of next year. The demand for news will escalate but may actually threaten a diminution in the ability of people to buy newspapers. Some shops now do not stock newspapers for fear of fighting over an insufficient supply. This is an unhealthy and potentially dangerous situation.

It is therefore urgently necessary to address the problems of supply and demand, the integrity of our press and its competence to provide people with information they will require to make informed decisions throughout this year and informed choices at the next election. Without accurate and untarnished information it is difficult for people to make correct decisions and this, at the end of the day, can damage the State.

5. Crisis

The crisis facing publications in general and Zimpapers in particular is mainly caused by shortage of newsprint, an imposed and unrealistic cover price, a controlled and unrealistic tariff and, in the case of the Chronicle, obsolete equipment. These are the major reasons why Zimpapers' profits dropped so dramatically by 93% last year.

In order to ensure that their newspapers can perform effectively editors must therefore take determined action to solve these problems by bringing them inescapably to the attention of the Government. For example it can be asked what logic there is in giving Bulawayo a new university and denying it a new press.

6. Integrity of the press

Recently the President stated that the people were crying for the blood of the leaders, and with due reason. An editor by virtue of the role he plays in society is a leader although I'm sure the President didn't have you in mind when he made this statement. But just as people demand and eventually get a certain standard in the conduct of Government, so people demand and eventually get a certain standard in the press that serves them. That's what the struggle for press freedom is all about. If the insecurity of editors makes it difficult to attain that standard then this situation must be redressed.

Questions that could be asked are, for example:

Is the constitutional right of the people of Zimbabwe to freedom of expression being fully enjoyed and properly safeguarded? If not, what can be done about this?

Who exactly appoints and promotes editors and what is the process of selection?

Is it in the interests of our newspaper industry to have the position of Chairman of the Board of Directors of Zimpapers held by the same person as is the Chairman of the Board of Trustees of the MMT?

In retrospect, can the acquisition by the MMT of over 50% of the shares in Zimpapers be seen as a positive step in the long run for the freedom of our press? If not, can there be pressure for the sale of those shares to the public perhaps with the proviso that the shares be sold only to Zimbabweans?

The preceding questions naturally relate forcibly to the position of editors within Zimpapers and their ability to perform their duty to the people, that duty being to provide information. You can see from the long, long queues for newspapers these days that people are starving for information, and their hunger must be satisfied.

I look forward to your comments although this letter is so limited in scope. To broaden the range of discussion you might raise these issues and others for readers in the pages of the Herald. On my part I'll send copies of this letter to a few people concerned such as some of our Members of Parliament. As this is an open letter they could in turn if they wanted make copies available to others and this would help facilitate a general debate on the press in Zimbabwe.

   With best wishes.

Yours sincerely,

Judith Todd

RECENT PUBLICATIONS

AFRICA WATCH REPORTS

News from Africa Watch, A frequent newsletter designed to provide up-to-the-minute information on human rights in Africa, $50.00 per year
Angola
Violations of the Laws of War by Both Sides, April 1989, 148 pages, $10.00
South Africa
No Neutral Ground — South Africa's Confrontation with the Activist Churches, August 1989, 145 pages, $10.00
The Persecution of Human Rights Monitors in South Africa, June 1988, 38 pages, $4.00

HUMAN RIGHTS WATCH REPORTS

Human Rights Watch Newsletter, designed to provide information on human rights developments worldwide. Published quarterly. $15.00 per year
Forced Out: The Agony of the Refugee in Our Time, April 1989, 191 pages, 189 black and white photographs, $19.95
Critique of the Department of State's Country Reports on Human Rights Practices for 1988 (Human Rights Watch/Lawyers Committee for Human Rights), July 1989, 216 pages, $15.00
The Persecution of Human Rights Monitors, December 1988, 217 pages, $15.00
The Reagan Administration's Record on Human Rights for 1988 (Human Rights Watch/Lawyers Committee), January 1989, 340 pages, $15.00
Annual Report of 1988, April 1989, 101 pages, Free